CW01650563

J Ward

SEPTEMBER 1972.

Studies in Sociology

Edited by

PROFESSOR W. M. WILLIAMS

University College, Swansea

1

THE SOCIOLOGY OF INDUSTRY

STUDIES IN SOCIOLOGY

Urban Sociology
by Professor R. N. Morris

The Family
by C. C. Harris

Demographic Analysis
by Bernard Benjamin

In preparation

Social Stratification
by James Littlejohn

Rural Sociology
by Professor W. M. Williams

Political Sociology
by Professor Philip Abrams

The Sociology of Education
by Professor M. P. Carter

The Sociology of Organizations
by Professor J. E. T. Eldridge and A. Crombie

Methodology of the Social Sciences
by Michael Lessnoff

The Sociology of Knowledge
by Sami Zubaide

Community Studies
by Colin Bell

The Sociology of Development
by Jamil Hillal

The Sociology of Religion
by Joan Brothers

THE SOCIOLOGY OF INDUSTRY

S. R. Parker
Government Social Survey

R. K. Brown
University of Durham

J. Child
London Graduate School of Business Studies

M. A. Smith
University of Salford

London
GEORGE ALLEN AND UNWIN LTD
RUSKIN HOUSE · MUSEUM STREET

FIRST PUBLISHED IN 1967
SECOND IMPRESSION 1968
THIRD IMPRESSION 1969
FOURTH IMPRESSION 1970
FIFTH IMPRESSION 1971
(with minor corrections and bibliographical updating)

This book is copyright under the Berne Convention. All rights are reserved. Apart from any fair dealing for the purposes of private study, research, criticism or review, as permitted under the Copyright Act, 1956, no part of this publication may be reproduced, stored in a retrieval system, or transmitted in any form or by any means, electronic, electrical, chemical, mechanical, optical, photocopying, recording or otherwise, without the prior permission of the copyright owner. Enquiries should be addressed to the publishers.

© *George Allen & Unwin Ltd, 1967*

Cloth Edition ISBN 0 04 300014 2
Paper Edition ISBN 0 04 300015 0

REPRODUCED AND PRINTED IN GREAT BRITAIN
in 10 on 11 point Plantin type
BY REDWOOD PRESS LIMITED
TROWBRIDGE & LONDON

CONTENTS

Note:
The names against chapter titles indicate who was responsible for preparing the first drafts. All four authors took part subsequently in the process of revision and of integrating the chapters according to an agreed framework. However, the views expressed in each chapter remain the responsibility of its original author, and those of S. R. Parker do not represent the views of the Government Social Survey.

INTRODUCTION

THIS book is addressed mainly to students of sociology who are especially interested in its application to the 'world of work'. It is intended as an introduction, but assumes that the reader is not completely unfamiliar with the sociological approach to the study of society. The purpose of the book is twofold: to synthesize the growing body of relevant empirical material, and to show how sociological theory at different levels of analysis treats the three interrelated aspects of the subject matter. It is these three interrelated aspects which constitute the three sections of the book.

The first section is at the social system level of analysis, and examines the relationship between industry and other sub-systems of society. These sub-systems are historically unique in structure, and in function have specific relationships which limit generalization. Consequently, we examine both the particular and general aspects of sub-systems and their relationships. We discuss specifically education, the family and the polity as sub-systems each of which affects industry and is affected by it. At this level, industrial sociology forms part of a wider economic sociology, which is the application of the general frame of reference, variables and explanatory models of sociology to the complex of activities concerned with production, distribution, exchange and consumption.[1] However, the purely economic aspects of these activities, which form the subject matter of theoretical and applied economics, are outside the scope of this book.

The second part of the book, constituting the second level of analysis, is concerned with the internal structure of industry and the roles which individuals play in that structure. Organization theory is the link between systems analysis and work organizations. Our concern, therefore, is with attempts to define organizational structures and processes. Particular attention is given to authority and technology as aspects of work organizations. These include the structure of management, informal organization, technology and technical change, and some key problems in industrial relations between management and unions. Again, the emphasis is on knitting aspects of sociological theory with historical and functional aspects of the structure of industrial organization.

In that structure itself is concerned with relations between roles and

[1] N. J. Smelser: *The Sociology of Economic Life*, Englewood Cliffs: Prentice-Hall, 1963, p. 32.

variations in kinds of roles it is closely bound up with the third major level of analysis dealt with in the third part of the book, namely, work and non-work roles of individuals. This final part corresponds to what is sometimes defined as the sociology of occupations and, apart from describing some of the main features of the labour force, includes an analysis of work roles, adjustments to these roles by occupational groups and the interaction between work and non-work life of particular types of individual.

Distinction of the subject matter of industrial sociology in terms of the institution-system level, organization-role level, and role-person level has been made with two main considerations in mind. Firstly, the theoretical framework must be congruent with a sociological perspective applicable to other fields of analysis. Secondly, existing empirical and theoretical contributions to the field of industrial sociology require a logical form permitting consistent analysis of levels of contribution and identification of levels of problems. This second consideration may lead us sometimes to point out that research is lacking or inadequate in some areas. Also, relating a large amount of material to a theoretical framework can over-simplify the complexity of the phenomena; indeed it would be surprising if the logical framework did not result in some boundary distortion and theoretical or empirical simplification.

Three further points may be noted. Firstly, the higher the level of abstraction the more likely the analysis is to be functionalist[2] and to admit historical variation. Secondly, there is no assumption of simple causal relationships between variables, whether they are defined as system, structural or behavioural. And thirdly, induction and deduction—how to move from the particular to the general and from the general to the particular—have been dealt with in a variety of ways, and in this sense the second section of the book is the key one for integrating perspectives from general theory and the 'person' level of analysis.

No one who sets out to write a book on sociology organized around a theoretical framework succeeds entirely in relating all his material to that framework, and we are no exceptions. Although we have tried to include some consideration of what seem to us to be the more important research findings and theories, inevitably in a book of this small size and large scope the treatment of each topic is brief. The interested reader will, however, be able to follow up particular topics through the references given and the suggested reading.

[2] This does not commit us to uncritical acceptance of any particular 'functionalist' theory of society.

1

Scope and Directions in Industrial Sociology

SOCIOLOGY is concerned with the systematic study of social relationships and with the interaction between social structure and the behaviour of individuals and groups. The adjective 'industrial' implies the application of sociological theories and methods to one segment of society, that is, the one concerned with the economic function of producing and distributing the goods and services which society requires. Industry is sometimes narrowly defined as what takes place in factories, but in this book we shall use it to mean the world of work. Thus industry encompasses not only the factory but also the farm, the office, the school and the hospital, insofar as these are settings in which work takes place and goods are produced or services rendered.

The central concern in this introductory chapter is the relationship of general sociology to industrial sociology. We examine this relationship from two aspects: (1) we see the aims and content of industrial sociology as a specific perspective of general sociology, and (2) we consider the theoretical assumptions and methods common to fields of sociological analysis.

AIMS AND CONTENT

Sociology endeavours to formulate generalizing statements into a logically consistent body of theory and to derive postulates from that theory which can be verified by particular methods. How theory is built is not a problem which can be dealt with here but, depending upon the starting point of analysis, either classificatory or constructual concepts are defined.[1] Sociology is moving away from thinking that any one level of analysis is sufficient, and tends now to relate both system and

[1] Classificatory concepts are *logically* consistent, whereas constructual concepts are *empirically* adequate.

behaviour aspects of society by the organization-role level of analysis.[2]

Sociology and industrial sociology share the same general aim. In terms of *what* they are concerned to generalize about, however, they are different. Sociology is concerned to examine all aspects of social systems, their structures and functions, and the processes which relate types of system to types of structure and types of structure to types of function. The interest is in how systems, structure, functions and processes combine to produce social action and relate to social interaction within a framework of roles and norms.

Industrial sociology is concerned with how the economic sub-system is related to other sub-systems, how that sub-system is structured in terms of particular work organizations and roles, and how persons fit into those roles. This can be usefully spelt out systematically. The economic sub-system interacts with other sub-systems in a total social system. The social system comprises the familial, political, educational, stratification and other sub-systems, which are variously related to the economic sub-system. Sociology is concerned with all aspects of sub-system structures, functions and processes and their inter-relationships, and the economic sub-system is part of this concern. Each sub-system has two general dimensions of analysis, the institutional and the organizational. The institutional dimension concerns the established norms and structures which govern the behaviour of large social groups. Institutionalization, therefore, refers to the process by which the social structure becomes stable and individuals 'internalize' its norms and values. The organizational dimension refers to the *power* structure of social systems and concerns the extent to which particular roles and situational circumstances combine to pattern behaviour.

Sociology is concerned with these dimensions in all sub-systems, while industrial sociology is concerned with them particularly in the economic sub-system. This sub-system analysis forms the first part of the book. The important point to grasp here is that industrial sociology is closely related to general system analysis because work organizations are the particular dimension of the economic sub-system, organizations in general being one dimension of all sub-system analysis. Sociology is concerned with this structuring of sub-systems in two senses—historically and functionally. Both are necessary for adequate definition and analysis of organizations, in industrial as well as general sociology.

Organizations possess an internal aspect and consist of persons behaving in accordance (more or less) with the expectations and

[2] Talcott Parsons, *Structure and Process in Modern Societies*, Glencoe: Free Press, 1960, esp. Part 1.

demands of the positions they occupy. The second part of the book is concerned with how this internal structure has been thought of. What is done by persons in particular positions is of general concern in all types of organizations. Industrial sociology specifically analyses the content of work roles, the norms or expectations associated with the *same* work roles in different work organizations and *different* work roles in the same organization. It is also concerned with the 'compliance' structure of work organizations as it relates roles to each other and persons to roles in a systematic way.

This distinction between the content of roles, orientation towards roles, and what persons actually do or how they behave in roles that are systematically related, shows that industrial sociology, in its analysis of work roles, is one application of role theory. Variations in orientation towards the work role and the effect which types of work role have for the non-work life of persons, is the third aspect of analysis with which industrial sociology is concerned; it includes themes which are also of concern to sociology in general: alienation and the nature of identity; the relationship between socialization, motivation and rational, non-rational and irrational action; and the fit between dimensions of personality and dimensions of roles.

Thus far it has been suggested that the claim of industrial sociology to be an independent sub-section of general sociology cannot be supported by distinctions between the general aims and content. But before the second aspect (the theoretical assumptions and methods which both share) is examined, it would be useful to re-state the three interrelated aspects of our definition of the subject matter. Industrial sociology consists of the application of the methods and models of sociology to the analysis of work organizations and work roles. Work organizations are a particular aspect of the structuring of the economic sub-system; this sub-system is variously related to other sub-systems, while organizations are internally structured by systematically related roles. Work roles are objectively defined as an aspect of organizations, and subjectively defined as how persons orient towards work roles and what they do in those roles. What persons do and how they perceive the work role variously relates to non-work roles and the salience of non-work life areas.

ALTERNATIVE FORMULATIONS

It is instructive to compare this initial formulation of the subject matter with others which have been put forward. J. H. Smith has defined the field of industrial sociology as 'the study of social relations in industrial and organizational settings, and of the way these relations influence and are influenced by, relations in the wider community.'[3] Lupton has been more specific and advanced 'the study of the social system of the factory and of the influences external to the factory which affect that system.'[4] Etzioni has suggested that industrial sociology can be fruitfully conceived of as a branch of organizational sociology,[5] while Nosow and Form believe that occupational sociology forms an independent sub-field within industrial sociology.[6] All these definitions have some inadequacies. The first is too general and the second too particular. To think of industrial sociology as an aspect of organizational theory because certain types of organizations have common functional problems ignores the historical differences between organizations and the fact that there are aspects of industrial sociology which are not concerned with organizations.

Nosow and Form have claimed that occupational sociology is a distinct field within industrial sociology. The claim deserves attention and rests on their identification of five major themes which occupational sociology has dealt with: the social nature of work and related phenomena such as leisure, retirement and unemployment; analysis of the occupational structure; the study of individual occupations; analysis of how the occupational structure and individual occupations relate to other aspects of the social structure; and the study of a particular occupation to highlight a social problem. The claim that occupational sociology can form a distinct level of enquiry is only tenable if the content and variations of work roles are not systematically related to dimensions of organizations within which they occur. The absence of any consistent and united perspective in organizational theory has increased the stress upon an occupational level of analysis, but in our opinion it is unfortunate that the two have been pursued independently. One of the main objectives of this volume is to show that they are *interdependent* dimensions and, as Schneider has put it, industrial sociology is a particular level from which generalizations applicable to sociology in general are derived, as well as to which they are applied.[7]

Since Schneider's is one of the most insightful of recent contribu-

[3] *The University Teaching of Social Sciences: Industrial Sociology*, UNESCO 1961, p. 31.

[4] *Ibid.*

[5] A. Etzioni, 'Industrial Sociology: the Study of Economic Organizations', *Social Research*, Autumn, 1958.

[6] S. Nosow and W. H. Form, *Man, Work and Society*, New York: Basic Books, 1962, p. 3.

[7] E. V. Schneider, *Industrial Sociology*, New York: McGraw-Hill, 1957, p. 5.

tions to the field, it is useful to note that the definition of sociology as a specializing and generalizing social science accords well with the preliminary definition already outlined. Schneider regards sociology as specializing in certain areas which other social sciences either ignore or treat as peripheral to their main interests. For example, the informal group in industry is treated as a counterpart of the clique or gang found in the wider society, and the social structure of industry is treated as a type of organization. As a generalizing science, sociology is concerned with the structure, functions and processes of groups and organizations in general. Thus the sociologist may consider industrial conflict or trade union organization as examples of social processes, or he may recognize in the industrial setting types of action—rational, affective, tradition-directed or idealistic—which are found in all kinds of situations.

The *scope* of industrial sociology may be considered in terms of the three levels of analysis already dealt with. The *directions* of enquiry have not always consistently reflected these dimensions. The fields in which studies of industrial sociology have been made, however, may be divided into five main areas:

(1) analysis of 'bureaucratized' industry from the point of view of organizational roles and the behaviour and attitudes of professional and blackcoated workers,

(2) studies of workplaces as complex organic or socio-technical systems by which individuals achieve some balance between the demands of the work situation and their own goals,

(3) studies of working groups (mainly informal) and their systems of relationships, aims and beliefs, particularly where these contrast with those of management,

(4) analysis of the 'industrial relations' complex—mainly descriptions of the historical development of labour organizations, bargaining procedures and types of trade unions,

(5) analysis of the consequences of industrialism for the individual, including the interaction between work and non-work areas of life.

Examples of studies in each of these areas are given in a review of industrial sociology by Burns, of which the above is a summary.[8] The amount of attention given to each of these areas has been unequal, mainly because much research has been problem-oriented without a systematic attempt having been made to relate the nature of the problem to a general theoretical perspective. In the words of W. H. Scott, 'the field is still beset by a rather high proportion of superficial reports

[8] T. Burns, 'The Sociology of Industry', in A. T. Welford (ed.), *Society: Problems and Methods of Study*, London: Routledge, 1962.

and, indeed, uncompleted projects—in the sense that they have not issued in publications of academic status which enable the work to be utilized by other research workers.'[9] The small number of sociologists compared to 'management theorists' and human relations experts has also led to the uneven development of research.

The five directions of enquiry noted by Burns can be used to indicate the directions of change which to some extent are reflected in the approach adopted by contributors to this volume. Analysis of bureaucratization of industrial organization has made some progress in explaining the internal structure of work organizations and attention is now starting to turn from exploring the process and consequences of bureaucratization to the *comparative* analysis of institutionalized procedures and organizations, some of which are traditional and non-rational. This comparative approach means looking at differences between types of organizations and is an aspect of organization theory. Studies of the 'factory' and work organizations within a localized framework are moving towards a systematic view of the way work roles are structured and of the way in which work organizations 'process' their members. The problem is how far roles are objectively or subjectively determined and how work and non-work roles are related.

The relationship between work behaviour and the norms which regulate interaction in the work situation has usually been examined by looking at the ways in which informal work groups seek to behave independently of the formal structure. Again, this is an aspect of how various types of roles within the work organization structure members' interaction and how those who occupy the roles *perceive* the organizational—usually authority—structure. The industrial relations complex has been composed of a variety of case studies of strikes, types of issues in industrial conflict, and particularly the part played by trade unions and professional associations. Since the bargaining procedure is an aspect of the normative framework which governs the relations between shop floor and management, this is an organization-role problem. Trade unions and professional associations are examples of secondary work organizations and are therefore best treated as part of the organization of the economic sub-system. Finally, the study of particular occupations has included research on mine-workers, fishermen, clerks, dock workers, steelworkers and others. These are all work roles and can be systematically analysed into the objective and subjective aspects of such roles. The five areas which Burns outlines deal with overlapping aspects of the subject matter of

[9] W. H. Scott, 'The Aims of Industrial Sociology', *British Journal of Sociology* Sept. 1959.

industrial sociology, and can be systematically related in the framework already outlined.

ASSUMPTIONS AND METHODS

There is one theoretical problem which concerns all the social sciences. It is the relationship between 'how we know' and 'what we mean', or the problem of validating empirical relationships and defining the concepts used to isolate the content of variables. *Validity* is treated by the use of the comparative, statistical and observation-experiment methods. The assumption is that the objectivity of method, and the quantification it permits, make sociology scientific. The theoretical framework used in sociology is broader than those enjoined by the methods noted. The problem, however, is that this framework has to be applied to phenomena which are normative, or within a particular framework of values. The *assumption* is that the methods used in sociology do verify empirical relationships; the *problem* is whether behaviour which is intrinsically normative can be objectively treated and subjected to predictive analysis.

The problem of defining the empirical content and boundaries of concepts has been regarded as a logical problem, or one of formulating the content of the subject matter so that it is susceptible to deduction. Those theorists who start from the system concept have to show how it is possible to move from this level of abstraction to social behaviour. The usual consequence of starting from the system level has been a deductive typology which is difficult to operationalize. This has meant using classificatory concepts, since these meet the requirement of logical consistency. Alternatively, those theorists who have started from the level of behaviour have had the problem, which they have not usually solved satisfactorily, of induction to a general of analysis.

These two types of concept, classificatory and constructual, have been used to generalize from the particular and particularize the general. They have also been put forward in an attempt to make the concepts used in sociology objective. The success in this second respect can be said to be fairly substantial, since such concepts as system, structure, role, function and process do not presume any particular value orientation.[10] The deduction-induction problem has, however, been less easily resolved, and few attempts have been made to treat both ways of defining concepts within the same general perspective. This problem has not been helped by the extent to which each way

[10] This does not preclude the study of the effect of different value-orientations on social structure and behaviour.

of defining concepts and relating them to different levels of abstraction has resulted in a functional analysis and a historical orientation respectively. In that sociology is now concentrating on a middle range of theory and a structural-functional approach, the definition of the scope and directions of industrial sociology reflects these changes: it is an attempt to treat theoretical problems and assumptions by the analysis of work organizations and work roles, as well as integrating perspectives in industrial sociology.

2

The Structure of the Economy

THE highest level of abstraction used in sociological analysis involves the concept of a *social system*. At this societal level we are concerned with the different needs, purposes and types of activity which the community as a whole shows and with how these mesh with each other. The system itself may be classified by one or more of its main features compared with those of other systems. Thus, for example, according to the Marxian analysis of stages of society the type of economic structure or mode of production has historically taken several forms, of which the capitalist form is the most recent in the industrially advanced areas of the world. For present purposes we shall assume a type of system corresponding to what is often called modern industrial society, since political differences in the structure of particular modern industrial societies are not crucial to the analysis.

According to Talcott Parsons, all social systems have to solve four basic problems of needs: (1) *adaptation*: the accommodation of the system to the reality demands of the environment coupled with the active transformation of the external situation; (2) *goal achievement:* the defining of objectives and mobilization of resources to attain them; (3) *integration*: establishing and organizing a set of relations among the member units of the system that serve to co-ordinate and unify them into a single entity; and (4) *latency*: the maintenance over time of the system's motivational and cultural patterns.[1] Smelser suggests that, from the point of view of society as a whole, certain sub-systems or institutions have the function of meeting these needs: the *economic* system of meeting adaptive needs, the *political* system of meeting goal achievement needs, *solidary* groupings such as the family or ethnic group of meeting integrative needs, and the *cultural* system of meeting

[1] T. Parsons *et al., Working Papers in the Theory of Action,* Glencoe: Free Press, 1953, pp. 183–6.

the needs of latency (earlier called pattern maintenance and tension management).[2] As Devereux remarks, the fit between these basic system problems and institutions is far from perfect,[3] but Smelser points out that the classification of social structures involves assigning *primacy* of function only. Thus, for example, the religious structure has a 'political' aspect, an 'economic' aspect, and so on.[4]

At this point it is necessary to say something about the scope of economic and sociological analysis and the extent to which they overlap. Economics consists of the intensive study of one type of function in, or sub-system of, society: that of producing, distributing and exchanging goods and services. This is also the subject-matter of one branch of sociology, namely economic sociology, but in a way less specific to economics and more general to social institutions. The motives of individuals and groups and social processes are the concern of sociology; it is the specific effects of these motives and processes on the production and use of different goods and services that fall within the province of economics. Economic sociology itself deals on the one hand with the social institutions of the economic system, their specific location and historical structure, and on the other hand with social influences on economic behaviour.[5]

The concept of system can be applied at levels other than the societal level. It is possible to view the economy as the parent system which itself consists of a number of component parts or sub-systems. Each of these component parts bears the same functional relation to the economic system as this bears to the social system as a whole. Thus it has been suggested that there is capitalization and investment (adaptation), production, including distribution and sales (goal-achievement), organization, including the entrepreneurial function (integration), and physical, cultural and motivational resources (latency).[6] Further, a more concrete structure, such as a market or a firm, may be analysed in a similar way.

In the rest of this chapter we shall deal with the present state of, and recent changes in the economic sub-system in Britain. In subsequent chapters in this part we shall examine the interrelation of the economy with other sub-systems of society.

[2] N. J. Smelser, *The Sociology of Economic Life*, Englewood Cliffs: Prentice-Hall, 1963, pp. 39–64.

[3] E. C. Devereux in M. Black (ed.), *The Social Theories of Talcott Parsons*, Englewood Cliffs: Prentice-Hall, 1961, p. 61.

[4] N. J. Smelser, *op. cit.*, p. 28.

[5] A. Loewe, *Economics and Sociology*, London: Allen and Unwin, 1935, p. 31.

[6] T. Parsons and N. J. Smelser, *Economy and Society*, London: Routledge, 1956, p. 44.

CHANGES IN THE ECONOMIC STRUCTURE

In an exploratory study of the sociology of the economy, some middle course must be steered between a static view of the economy as it is today and a long historical view going back at least to the beginning of the Industrial Revolution in this country. For purposes of empirical research it is often unavoidable to take a static view of some feature of economic behaviour or structure, but the researcher must be wary of generalizing the findings to other times and places in which they might not hold good. Thus although most economists treat both employment opportunities and supply of labour offered as mainly functions of price, where social prestige factors make leisure preferable to work price changes may have a negligible influence on labour supply.[7] But strictly speaking the view of the economic structure over time is primarily the province of the economic historian and the view over space (beyond modern industrial societies) the province of the social anthropologist. Accordingly, we shall concentrate on both a static and dynamic analysis of some of the main present features of, and trends of change in the economic structure in twentieth century Britain.

Two of the basic units of social structure are *roles,* or the parts that individuals play as a result of occupying some position or status in society (e.g. employee, business man) and *organization,* which refers to structured clusters of roles (e.g. a bureaucracy, a firm). To these two concepts we may add *technology,* or the application of scientific principles to the achievement of particular ends.

Technology

Our first theme under the general heading of technology is the growing importance of industrial as against agricultural activities. In 1851 agriculture and fisheries accounted for 22% of the occupied population in Britain; the proportion fell to 8% in 1911, 5% in 1951 and is now about 4%.[8] Structural changes in the economy may be measured either by such changes in the distribution of the working population or by censuses of production, which take into account greater productivity achieved by the substitution of machines and processes for workers. Thus between 1907 and 1948 the output of all factory trades rose by 146% but that of mining and quarrying was down by a fifth.[9]

[7] S. Rottenberg, 'Income and Leisure in an Underdeveloped Economy', *Journal of Political Economy*, Apr. 1952, p. 101.

[8] G. C. Allen, *The Structure of Industry in Britain*, London: Longmans, 1961, pp. 8, 219.

[9] K. S. Lomax, 'Production and Productivity Movements in the U.K. since 1900', *Journal of the Royal Statistical Society*, Vol. 122, Part 2, 1959.

New inventions and technological advances and shifts in world demand have altered radically the character of British industry. Industries in which new techniques have predominated, notably electronics, aircraft, motor and chemicals industries, new branches of machinery construction, and petroleum are contributing a significantly larger share of the total output and of total exports and providing wider employment opportunities for an increasingly skilled labour force.

Our second theme concerns the increasing application of technological methods in industry. Expenditure on industrial and scientific research has increased steadily and facilities for technical education have been greatly enlarged. But the existence of inventive genius and organized research is only one factor in what Florence calls the self-perpetuating 'circular' character of the train of causation.[10] Certain material, product and market conditions are necessary for inventive genius or organized research to have affected production. Although it is often said that we are entering an atomic age, technology does not move forward evenly over industry as a whole.[11] Automatic factories already exist in such industries as chemicals and engineering; the construction industry is closer to the craft age, though prefabricated factory building is on the increase.

Thirdly, there is the question of *values*, which provide the rationale for particular norms or rules of organization or conduct. Appropriate values are equally necessary with material conditions to enable a certain kind of social and economic system to be developed and to operate. Modern industrial society has come to assign to economic productivity a very high value indeed. The need to maximise profits or wages and the need to work hard reflect values peculiar to our own and closely related societies; such values are found only rarely in other parts of the world.[12] The utilization of science for technical organization and industrial production is an aspect of culture which has been of profound importance in shaping the character of modern industry. That science ought, sooner or later, to be useful is a widespread belief in our society, and contemporary industrial technology represents one fulfilment of that conviction.[13] It may be added that the

[10] P. S. Florence, *Economics and Sociology of Industry*, London: Watts and Co., 1964.

[11] D. C. Miller, 'Influence of Technology on Industry' in F. R. Allen *et al.* (eds.), *Technology and Social Change*, New York: Appleton-Century-Crofts, 1957, p. 266.

[12] E. V. Schneider, *Industrial Sociology*, New York: McGraw-Hill, 1957, p. 13.

[13] W. E. Moore, *Industrial Relations and the Social Order*, New York: Macmillan, 1946, p. 46.

extension of scientific methods and theories into the fields of human behaviour itself represents a value choice that it is better to study society scientifically than in some other way.

Values differ from society to society, and *within* societies there may be different sub-cultures and therefore different prevailing values in each. The sub-cultures of management and labour are different enough for these two groups to possess somewhat different values toward each other's roles. Inconsistent general values may be contained within the same society, provided that they are 'rendered compatible by their distribution among various statuses in the social structure so that they do not result in conflicting demands upon the same persons at the same time'.[14]

Organization

During the past hundred years or so the British economy has shown an expansion in industrial output and an increase in imports; the economy has become increasingly differentiated and specialized as a manufacturing unit.[15] The process of differentiation of goods produced and services offered has also been accompanied by the localizing of particular industries.[16]

Part of the process of development of the economy is the trend towards increasing size of industrial factories or plants. Over industry as a whole, from employing in 1935 roughly one-third of all persons in each of the three main sizes of plant, Britain in 1959 had almost twice as many in plants employing 500 or more than in those employing under 100.[17] Those figures refer to size of plant, or unit of continuous building; the trend in the size of firm is more difficult to determine. The majority of business enterprises remain small and unincorporated; of the 56,000 manufacturing establishments in 1959, at least 40,000 employed fewer than 100 people, while fewer than 3,000 employed more than 500 people.[18] The size of units is limited in some industries by the conditions of production and in others by the character of demand. Thus in building repair work and in much road haulage the output is scattered and erratic, while in other industries

[14] R. K. Merton, *Social Theory and Social Structure*, Glencoe: Free Press, 1957, p. 502.

[15] P. S. Florence, *op. cit.*, p. 18.

[16] For details see *ibid.*, esp. Chapter 3.

[17] *Ibid.*, p. 78.

[18] J. W. Grove, *Government and Industry in Britain*, London: Longmans, 1962, p. 65.

small-scale operations occur where firms make types of product for which demand is limited.[19]

Another trend in industry is the growing proportion of organizers, managers, and research, technical and administrative staff compared to actual working operatives. The ratio of staff to operatives in British manufacturing industry has risen from 11·8% in 1924 to 26·1% in 1957.[20] American evidence is that staff has increased less than the rise in productivity level. This probably holds good for Britain and is a consequence of increased output due to the use of machines which displace the operative but add to the work of staff. This trend toward higher staff ratios is likely to continue with the increasing application of science and greater forward planning, budgeting, and other management procedures.

A well-known theme which has been much discussed since the pioneer work of Berle and Means[21] is the alleged divorce of ownership from control of companies. In his book *The Managerial Revolution*, Burnham put forward the theory that effective economic control has passed out of the hands of owners and into those of professional management.[22] The weaknesses of his 'theory' are that he makes assumptions rather than demonstrations of the changes he alleges have taken place, his definition of 'managers' is not consistent, and he sometimes appears to call managers simply those who are powerful.[23] However, his basic point that the class structure of the industrial enterprise is based on authority and not directly on legal ownership is sound.

On a more empirical level, Florence made a study of nearly 300 large companies and concluded that two-thirds were probably not owner-controlled, i.e. a small proportion of the ordinary shares were owned by boards as a whole and a small number of directors were among the largest twenty shareholders.[24] But these conclusions have been disputed. Barratt Brown argued that the spread of share ownership actually increases the power of large shareholders on boards, and

[19] D. Burn (ed.), *The Structure of British Industry: A Symposium*, Vol. II, Cambridge: University Press, 1958, p. 441.

[20] P. S. Florence, *op. cit.*, p. 15.

[21] A. A. Berle and G. C. Means, *The Modern Corporation and Private Property*, New York: Macmillan, 1933, pp. 70f.

[22] J. Burnham, *The Managerial Revolution*, New York: John Day, 1941.

[23] A balanced assessment of Burnham's theory in relation to wider Marxian theories of society can be found in R. Dahrendorf's *Class and Class Conflict in Industrial Society*, London: Routledge, 1959, pp. 87–91.

[24] P. S. Florence, *Ownership, Control and Success of Large Companies*, London: Sweet and Maxwell, 1961, p. 185.

that a resolute person or group can win control with only 10% holding.[25] He also traced the interlocking directorships of 400 top controllers in banking, insurance, industry, commerce and the government. In one sense, however, the managerial revolution *has* taken place: the role of the financier is less important in industry with increasing profit plough-back. The executive director, often an engineer or accountant, has become relatively more important.

One important consequence of the increasing size of industrial organizations is the trend to monopoly or oligopoly. According to Aaronovitch, the 'big fifty club' of companies earned one-third of all profits (excluding finance and agriculture) in 1950.[26] Capitalism has always been in a contradictory position on monopolies: they have economic advantages resulting from larger markets, can enable production to be rationalized, but are also 'in restraint of trade'. Despite legislation against them, they still flourish in Britain and America. Mennell has made a study of the latest monopoly technique—the takeover. He describes how this process has speeded up in recent years. Of the 100 largest companies in 1954, one was taken over by 1957, but eight more by 1961.[27] One consequence of takeovers is to concentrate ownership and control even further; also they often have the personally unfortunate effect of losing people their jobs through redundancy.

A question to ask when considering the structure of the economy is: who owns the wealth of the country? It is sometimes asserted that increasing taxation has narrowed the gap between the property owners and the propertyless, but the facts do not bear this out. Before the last war, 2% of the adult population had £5,000 or more, equal to 66% of the total wealth. In 1946–50, 1½% had £10,000 or more (the rough equivalent of £5,000 pre-war), equal to 54% of the total wealth.[28] However, income is more evenly distributed: the top half million (or roughly 2% of all) income earners took in 1955 only 12% of the total personal income before tax, compared with 21% taken by this group in 1938.[29] The changes in distribution of income which have taken place as a result of increased and differential taxation are diffi-

[25] M. Barratt Brown, 'The Controllers', *Universities and Left Reiew*, Autumn 1958 Spring and Autumn 1959.

[26] S. Aaronovitch, *Monopoly: A Study of British Monopoly Capitalism*, London: Lawrence and Wishart, 1955, p. 44.

[27] W. Mennell, *Takeover: The Growth of Monopoly in Britain 1951-61* London: Lawrence and Wishart, 1962, p. 21.

[28] A. M. Carr-Saunders *et al.*, *A Survey of Social Conditions in England and Wales*, London: Oxford University Press 1958, p. 177.

[29] *Ibid*, 151.

cult to measure, but clearly those with very high gross incomes now retain proportionately less than they did pre-war.

The organization of industry and its effect on the economy as a whole, particularly in regard to labour matters, has been much influenced in post-war years by the growing power and authority of workers organized in trade unions. During the war trade unionists sat with employers' representatives on joint production committees in many industries, and the Trades Union Congress was called upon to play an important part in the formulation of economic policy. The gradual relaxation of wartime controls over labour and industrial relations left the trade unions in a far stronger position than ever before. Trade union leaders were appointed to the boards and commissions responsible for industries brought under public ownership, and union membership has risen to its present figure of ten million. Trade unions have grown into large, national, relatively tightly organized bodies. Industry has become more complex and concentrated, and the parts of the economy more interdependent, thus giving union action wider repercussions.

The Social Consequences of Full Employment

In an article written in 1943 Joan Robinson forecast some economic consequences of continued full employment into peacetime, assuming also a continuation of free wage-bargaining: '... there would be a constant upward pressure upon money wage-rates... It would greatly complicate the problem of controlling international trade, since it would require offsetting movements in exchange rates. It would make hay of the social security programme. It would bring about an arbitrary redistribution of real income within the country, *rentiers*, salary-earners, and ill-organized workers losing relatively to the members of the strong trade unions, who would secure the greatest wage advances, and to the industrialists, who could recoup themselves for rising costs by rising prices. Finally, if it moved too fast, it might precipitate a violent inflation.' [30] Most of this has come true, at least to some extent. Certain developments have, of course, modified some of the predictions; for example the setting up of international financial institutions, such as the International Monetary Fund and the Bank of International Settlements, has enabled exchange rates to remain comparatively stable. But beyond such economic considerations as these, what social consequences can be traced of a continuation of full employment, and the periodic emergence of what is sometimes called over-

[30] J. Robinson, *Collected Economic Papers*, Oxford: Blackwell, 1951, p. 85.

full employment (that is, an excess of vacancies over persons seeking employment)?

An expanding economy and the stronger market position of workers vis-à-vis employers has led to 'affluence' of the working class, at least relative to the poverty of many of its members before the war. Two developments have aided the expansion of the consumer market in post-war years: the growth of advertising and of hire-purchase sales. It was estimated that in 1965 about £590 million was spent on all forms of advertising in Britain, or about 2% of the total national income. The expansion of the teenage market for consumer goods and services, especially for clothes, records, and other products of the 'leisure' industries, is a direct result of the favourable market situation of most juvenile workers, with employers clamouring for their services and hence pushing up wage and salary rates. Although a circular process of demand and supply of labour and commodities is involved, the consumer is by no means the key factor in the situation. Rather, it is the producer who as a rule initiates economic change and consumers are educated by him if necessary; they are, as it were, brought to want new things.

The rapid growth of sales of household and durable consumer goods has been greatly helped in recent years by instalment purchasing. Despite fluctuations caused by intermittent government regulation of the terms of hire-purchase and credit sales agreements in order to help boost or damp down the economy, the total hire-purchase debt outstanding shows a strong upward trend. From about £490 million in 1958 it rose to nearly £1,200 million by mid-1966, falling somewhat in the subsequent recession. The need to keep up, and if possible expand demand for consumer goods has led to 'planned obsolescence' of products built not to last but to be replaced by later models more frequently than is really necessary. Obligations to repay hire-purchase debts have been said partly to account for an increasing tendency on the part of many workers to choose overtime rather than more leisure when basic working weeks are reduced.

Another consequence of full employment—labour mobility—will be dealt with in Chapter 12 from the point of view of the individual, but its relation to the needs of the economy may be briefly mentioned here. The main movement in population in recent years has been towards S.E. England and the Midlands and away from Scotland, Wales and N.W. region. These changes reflect the rise and decline of industries: the contraction of coal-mining, shipbuilding and the textile industries, and the growth of the metal, vehicle, aircraft, electrical and similar industries. Labour mobility has two types of factor to overcome—value and material. The values of family ties and community attachment have militated against movement from areas of declining employment. Material incentives have, however, been given in the shape of housing facilities offered by private firms in areas where they have found it advantageous to set up factories, or by the development corporations of new towns.

Finally there is the question of the economic role of technical specialization of the labour force. The extended division of labour is a concomitant of the trend towards an increasing proportion of staff to operatives noted earlier. Moore raises a fundamental question in the economics of specialization: does the division of labour introduce simplification of tasks, or increase technical competence?[31] Actually it does both. On the one hand, skilled labour costs can be cut to a minimum by breaking down complex operations into easily learned component units, and the use of machines can reduce the dependence of the manufacturer upon a small number of skilled workers not easily replaced. On the other hand, the very complexity of modern industrial organization has increased rather than decreased the demand for *skilled* specialists needed for research, design, planning, co-ordination, and maintenance.

[31] W. E. Moore, *op. cit.*, p. 448, 1951 edn.

3

Industry and Education

THE relations between industry and education are reciprocal, and have consequences for the structure of both institutions. On the one hand, there are the demands of industry for trained workers, or for those sufficiently well educated to be suitable for appropriate training; on the other hand, industry itself has an educational 'sub-system', including apprenticeship and on-the-job training schemes of various kinds. For the individual there is the half-way stage between being a student and being a worker that is implicit in the provision by some employers of day-release and 'sandwich courses'. At the individual level there is also the transition from school to work, a process which may involve problems of role and status in a changed social and physical environment.

THE INFLUENCE OF INDUSTRY ON EDUCATION

One of the most obvious ways in which the world of work affects the world of learning is in the choice of subjects in schools and the ways in which these are taught. What is often called the vocational bias in education means that education is regarded as a direct preparation for a particular kind of occupation. Employers want a convenient method of sorting out suitable applicants for jobs; a paper qualification obtained by examination is one such method, and hence the school curriculum often tends to be treated simply as a means to examination success.

Several types of school have a vocational bias, in a direct or indirect sense. Technical schools, which are attended by only about 6% of the secondary level pupils in Britain, are designed to afford entry to skilled manual and some non-manual occupations. Secondary modern schools, which are attended by about three-quarters of children between eleven and fifteen, often have vocational courses which can sometimes be a greater source of interest than purely academic subjects, but in recent years there has been a move towards education for non-work life. Among secondary modern schools in Sheffield, Carter found that although some courses had a vocational bias the children were not conditioned to specific types of work, but their interests and aptitudes were encouraged in the light of opportunities of local employment.[1]

The 1944 Education Act, which legislated for secondary education for all, has formed the basis of subsequent educational policy. Three types of secondary school—modern, grammar and technical—were provided for, 'differentiated in terms of their curricula, but equal in prestige.' However, while it has been possible to achieve some degree of parity of conditions, the essential corollary 'parity of esteem' has been more elusive. As Banks remarks, 'parents are not likely to accord equal favour to all three types of secondary education while the grammar schools . . . still provide the chief avenue, within the State system of education, to occupations of the highest social and economic standing.'[2] The trend towards greater occupational rewards for educational qualifications has brought the educational system into closer relation with the occupational structure.

The functions of the school in vocational preparation have been listed by Thomas as follows: (1) eliminating economic barriers to extended schooling, (2) overcoming cultural inequalities in student backgrounds, (3) diversifying the school's programme, (4) promoting critical understanding of the occupational structure, (5) promoting a wider distribution of occupational values, (6) individual guidance and 'vocational articulation', and (7) providing vocational training facilities and programmes.[3] The last, and to some extent the third and sixth, of these functions are *manifest,* or intended by educators—the others are *latent,* in the sense that these are not the ostensible purposes of vocational education but are put forward by its proponents as possible resulting advantages.

Criticisms of the vocational bias in education have centred around a concern that the links between education and industry may be at the expense of the role of education in other spheres of life. Thus Bantock writes that 'one's feeling about the Crowther Report [on

[1] M. P. Carter, *Home, School and Work,* Oxford: Pergamon Press, 1962, p. 11.

[2] O. Banks, *Parity and Prestige in English Secondary Education,* London: Routledge, 1955, p. 7.

[3] L. G. Thomas, *The Occupational Structure and Education,* Englewood Cliffs: Prentice-Hall, 1956, pp. 446–62.

education between 15 and 18] is that the needs of the practical life and of vocationalism have taken up their abode unashamedly and that it is the element of humanization which has been forced into a corner of the living room, though the need to recognize its presence there has not been forgotten.'[4] There were similar reactions to the more recent Robbins Report on higher education. Mannheim and Stewart expressed their concern with the narrowness of vocational education thus: 'although it produces the necessary cogs and wheels in the social machine, specialist education disintegrates both the personality and the mental powers for understanding the human situation which has to be mastered.'[5] None of these criticisms affects the fact that the needs of the occupational world inevitably impinge on the educational world, though the extent to which this happens in different types of society may be the subject of comparative study.[6] The difference of opinion arises from value judgments, and centres on the relative weight that should be given to vocational and non-vocational education.

Technical Education

In the nineteenth century industry as a whole was apathetic and even hostile to technical education. The inferior prestige of science, and particularly technological studies, has acted as a brake on both the expansion of provision in science and technology and the attraction of students to such courses.[7] The low status of the scientist in industry was the result chiefly of the pre-eminence in the nineteenth century of mainly non-scientific industries and the perpetuation of the neglect of scientific instruction by recruitment and promotion policies. A major factor accounting for industry's lack of support for technical education has been the small proportion of technically qualified men in higher management. A study in 1956 showed that even in large companies there were proportionately more top-level managers with non-technical qualifications than with technical.[8]

Several factors have contributed to the post-war expansion in technical education. Successive economic crises and foreign competition in export markets have underlined the importance of the

[4] G. H. Bantock, *Education in an Industrial Society*, London: Faber, 1963, p. 114.

[5] K. Mannheim and W. Stewart, *An Introduction to the Sociology of Education*, London: Routledge, 1962, p. 161.

[6] H. Hans, *Comparative Education*, London: Routledge, 1961, p. 64.

[7] S. Cotgrove, *Technical Education and Social Change*, London: Allen and Unwin, 1958, p. 190.

[8] Acton Society Trust, *Management Succession*, London: the Trust 1956.

application of scientific methods to production, especially in the newer industries such as chemicals and engineering. Government-sponsored research organizations have played a part by demonstrating the practical value of research. The increase in the scale of industrial organizations has enabled the largest of them to undertake more research and training of personnel in various branches of science and technology. Employers' associations, though not teaching bodies, have in some cases concerned themselves closely with the development of education and training for management, including the technical side.

Technical education is extremely heterogeneous and is carried on in a variety of educational establishments. Apart from secondary technical schools, there are technical colleges, technical institutes, colleges of further education, schools of art and craft, and so on. In recent years a limited number of colleges of advanced technology have been established which run courses of a standard comparable with that of university degree courses and those are now mostly designated as universities. There are also new qualifications, such as the CNAA degrees. Technical colleges are organized in four tiers according to the nature of their work. Below the colleges of advanced technology, regional colleges do much similar work but also less advanced studies; below these, area colleges do mostly technician and craft works; and, at the bottom, the local colleges do only this low level work.[9]

One controversial question concerns how much technical training should be provided by firms and how much by outside educational bodies. Specific training for a single job peculiar to the work and processes of the firm is usually regarded as the responsibility of the firm. But it is argued that more general education and training not specifically limited to a single machine or process can and should be given outside the firm.[10] To a large extent, size of firm determines whether technical education or training is provided. In large firms work-based training schemes are feasible, but smaller firms without the necessary manpower and facilities are forced to rely on externally based arrangements. With technical training provided by firms there is also the problem of one firm 'poaching' the labour that another has had the expense of training.

The spread of automation is likely to have important effects both on technical training in particular and on education in general. Because of the complexity and abstractness of the new industrial techniques,

[9] A. Beveridge, *Apprenticeship Now*, London: Chapman and Hall, 1963, p. 114.
[10] P. F. R. Venables, *Technical Education*, London: Bell, 1956, p. 184.

a theoretical university education will increasingly tend to carry more weight than apprenticeship and 'on-the-job' training. One consequence of this is to make promotion from the shop floor more and more difficult and to reduce occupational and hence intra-generational social mobility.[11] Working foremen, with no more technical training than those they supervise, will tend to be replaced by the 'foremen, B.Sc.' who are beginning to feature in situations vacant advertisements.

THE INFLUENCE OF EDUCATION ON INDUSTRY

Educational and training courses which take place wholly or partly within the firm reflect to some extent the purposes and values which are attached to education in the wider society. Such courses, including the system of apprenticeship, together with the effect of a better-educated labour force on the composition and distribution of manpower resources, constitute the chief influences of education on the industrial world.

Apprenticeship

The system of apprenticeship has changed little since the Middle Ages when, as a paternalistic relationship between the craftsman and the trainee, it formed an integral part of the guild system. Today the paternalism has largely vanished, but many of the associated customs remain. Apprenticeships are served, mostly for periods of four or five years, from the ages of fifteen or sixteen. During that period the youth has a mixture of on-the-job and back-to-school training, for which there are no universal standards laid down and no terminal tests or examinations of competence required. Some employers train their apprentices well, while others do not. Some firms impose stringent intelligence and adaptability tests, while others take on a few lads because they have always had apprentices around the workshop. Although the 1965 Industrial Training Act provides for imposing training levies on entire industries (thereby making it less profitable for firms to 'buy' apprentices with higher wages as they emerge from training) there is no legal obligation on any employer to provide training. Small wonder that the apprenticeship system has been described by one critic as 'that makeshift, class-ridden, inadequate, anachronistic contract which perpetuates master-servant relationships and the confusion, if not the exploitation, of the young in a sphere which

[11] 'The Social Consequences of Automation', *International Social Science Bulletin*, No. 1, 1958, p. 14.

cries out for enlightened and flexible forms of occupational training for *all* young people'.[12]

An enquiry by Williams revealed that apprentices are rarely, if ever, actually *taught* their trade.[13] The system relies on skilled men to teach them, and many are not good teachers. Williams, among others, advocates admission to the ranks of skilled workers as a result of a test of competence instead of the passage of time. Another problem is that although apprentices theoretically emerge as skilled craftsmen much of the work they are put to would be regarded objectively as semi-skilled, because of the fragmentation of many industrial processes. Since the great need of industry is for semi-skilled technicians, the apprenticeship system encourages unrealistic and rigid job definitions.

A recent survey of apprentice technicians in a Home Counties technical college found that their biggest grumble was lack of opportunity to use their abilities.[14] Forty per cent thought they did not receive enough instruction at work, and nearly as many were dissatisfied with the instruction given. This was particularly so among those coming from smaller firms where facilities for instruction were likely to be poorer. The survey also tested attitude differences among the three types of apprentice—Ordinary National Certificate, Technical, and Craft, which represent levels of educational performance ranked in that order. The Craft apprentices were significantly less aware than the others that they had unused abilities, and attached less importance to promotion prospects. These findings support the thesis that levels of occupational aspiration and expected achievement are conditioned by educational attainment and subsequent type of course attended, involving its own style of socialization for work.

Day-Release and 'Sandwich' Courses

The academic side of apprenticeship consists of such arrangements as day-release to technical colleges or 'sandwich' courses. Both serve the function of filling in the gaps that most on-the-job training leaves. Day-release means that young workers are given time off from work—usually one day a week—to attend courses of study at technical colleges of various types. There are three main levels, leading to professional,

[12] P. Paterson, 'The Apprenticeship Scandal', *New Statesman*, Jan. 14, 1966.

[13] G. Williams, *Recruitment to Skilled Trades*, London: Routledge, 1957, p. 194.

[14] T. S. Chivers and S. R. Parker, 'The Apprentice Technician and His Job', *Industrial Society*, Oct. 1966.

technician and skilled craftsman occupations.[15] The purpose of the course largely determines its length, varying from three to five years at the technician and skilled craftsman level up to seven years or more for professional qualifications. The professional courses usually include one or two evenings' or Saturday morning attendance each week.

Day-release is generally assumed to be a privilege conferred on young employees—usually apprentices—at the discretion of their employer. But engineering craft apprentices in federated firms have the *right* to day-release for technical training up to eighteen—normally one day a week, payment to be made at the *time rate* of wages.[16] Release from engineering, shipbuilding and electrical goods industries accounts for more than a third of all release, and the next five industries giving release are (in decreasing order) building, public utilities and local government, chemicals, commercial, and professional occupations.[17] Industries which give relatively little day-release are generally either those which require little training of their workers, or which provide on-the-job training.

Venables discusses the reasons for the different degrees of support given to day-release by various industries. Where a high standard of technical skill and knowledge has been necessary to the survival of the industry, this motive has been powerful enough to compel educational progress. In such trades as service and distribution, however, the benefits to the employer are less tangible. Not only is working time lost. but the knowledge that many a competitor does not give release and that when the period of training is finished the youth may be attracted elsewhere are strong deterrents to day-release.

'Sandwich' courses are so called because 'layers' of full-time college study and industrial experience alternate over a period of years, for example, six months in industry succeeding six months in college for three or four years. Sandwich courses present many administrative difficulties on both the industrial and educational side and have been slow to develop. In 1959 it was estimated that there were fewer than 8,000 students on such courses in England and Wales.[18] As compared with day-release, sandwich courses give much better opportunities for integrating academic study with industrial practice, which is especially important in training for management.

[15] P. F. R. Venables, *op. cit.*, p. 112.
[16] A. Beveridge, *op. cit.*, p. 104.
[17] P. F. R. Venables, *op. cit.*, p. 110.
[18] P. F. R. Venables, *Sandwich Courses*, London: Parrish, 1959, p. 20.

Manpower and Education

Up to World War I there were three main groups in industry, corresponding to various phases of technical development: unskilled manual, skilled manual, and commercial and clerical personnel. In recent years machines have taken over much clerical work and the unskilled manual occupations contain a relatively smaller proportion of the labour force.[19] The distinction between manual and non-manual, which rests on the older and somewhat false distinction between workers by 'hand or by brain' is becoming blurred. We are moving towards having a labour force containing a broad stratum of semi-skilled workers doing varied work, and trained technical employees. Accordingly, it is claimed that vocational training for the mass of workers will have to be increasingly on the model of the semi-skilled technician.[20] Abstract and 'human relations' qualities will be more often required to organize and supervise the work.

The increasing displacement and occupational mobility of labour brought about by the introduction of new machines and techniques has special consequences for the education of employees. Narrow vocational education would need to be more and more postponed, and work and study periods would alternate throughout an individual's life, so that change of occupation at various ages would be possible. The consequent need for training and re-training would become great, and perhaps 'grow to such proportions and be so crucial for development that the major division of the labour force will be between teaching and non-teaching.'[21]

The reciprocal influence of education and industry is nowhere better illustrated than in the reasons which industry has for helping education. These have been candidly set out by the American National Industrial Conference Board:[22]

(1) Colleges and universities are responsible for a great deal of the basic research in the natural and social sciences, from which eventually flow new products, new insights into employee and consumer behaviour, and new techniques for solving business problems.

(2) A continuing supply is provided, at no direct cost to business, of trained manpower to fill executive and professional positions.

[19] G. Friedmann, *The Anatomy of Work*, London: Heinemann, 1961, p. 176.

[20] H. Schelsky, 'Technical Change and Educational Consequences', in A. H. Halsey *et al.*, *Education, Economy and Society*, Glencoe: Free Press, 1961.

[21] A. Hovne, 'Manpower Planning and the Restructuring of Education', *International Labour Review*, June 1964.

[22] *Industry Aid to Education*, New York: National Industrial Conference Board, 1965, pp. 5–7.

(3) Because of the high correlation between people's schooling and their income, consumer-product companies are interested in there being more better-educated people.
(4) Also, there are less tangible reasons, e.g. seeking to gain goodwill or preserve the free enterprise system.

In Britain there is a tendency for large companies to encourage their senior employees to send their children to public schools. Some firms (such as Shell) have established insurance schemes to help pay school fees.[23] Others (including Rolls-Royce and the Midland Bank) provide closed scholarships for employees' children. Still others make substantial contributions to the finances of public schools. Not only are private firms helping to subsidize the public schools, but they are also encouraging the science side to be developed. Industry has also given similar help to universities, with the emphasis less on social status and more on technical and managerial education.

SCHOOL AND WORK

Although, according to the plan of this book, the role-person level of analysis of the relation between industry and education should be deferred to Part Three, it seems more appropriate to deal with it here. The transition from school to work may be considered under two headings: the aspirations and expectations which school leavers have concerning the occupational world, including how they come to choose particular occupations, and the type of vocational guidance they may be given by various people or agencies.

Aspirations and Expectations

Schoolchildren form certain impressions of the occupational world from different sources. At school they pick up bits of information about various occupations, though this information may be a little more direct when the syllabus includes subjects such as current affairs or social studies. The family is often an important source of information (and sometimes misinformation) about jobs and of instilling, in varying degrees or not at all, a motivation for achievement.[24] Also, the mass media of communication may impart direct

[23] E. A. Johns, *The Social Structure of Modern Britain*, Oxford: Pergamon Press, 1965, p. 111.

[24] D. C. McClelland *et al.*, *Talent and Society*, New York: Van Nostrand, 1958, and subsequent articles. For a more general consideration of the stages of occupational choice, see E. Ginzberg *et al.*, *Occupational Choice: An Approach to a General Theory*, New York: Columbia University Press, 1951; and P. M. Blau *et al.*, 'Occupational Choice: A Conceptual Framework', *Industrial and Labour Relations Review*, 9, 1956.

information given by people interested in vocational guidance and may also convey impressions and stereotypes of occupational roles as portrayed in films and on television.[25]

Various studies have been concerned with how schoolchildren and young workers view aspects of the occupational world. A survey by Musgrove of boys and girls aged fourteen to twenty in a northern industrial region showed that work was instrumental for them, but for other than crudely material ends; it was referred to largely as a learning situation (in a broad sense) by both manual and non-manual employees.[26] Mapes and others, in a study of school-leavers' hopes, found 'a group of young people largely concerned with delayed rather than immediate rewards, somewhat depressed by the physical circumstances of the work situation in their area, keenly aware of the importance of social relationships, able to state their own recommended characteristics of an employer. . .'[27]

Hill's study of boys in fourteen maintained grammar schools in the Midlands showed that among the section who had not made up their minds on the choice of a career (56% of the total) the overwhelming majority were more interested in conditions of work and material rewards.[28] This is in line with the finding by Beardslee and O'Dowd that most American college students seem to be more concerned with the life-styles which occupational incomes can bring rather than with the character of the work itself.[29] They see an occupation mainly as a means of earning a mode of living and only secondarily as a set of skills and responsibilities.

Vocational Guidance

Vocational guidance should be distinguished from personnel selection. Vocational guidance means advising individuals on the choice of an occupation; personnel selection means the employer trying to choose the right individual for the job.[30] Although more

[25] M. L. DeFleur, 'Occupational Roles as Portrayed on Television', *Public Opinion Quarterly*, Spring, 1964, who claims these portrayals are 'selective, unreal, stereotyped and misleading.'

[26] F. Musgrove, *The Family, Education and Society*, London: Routledge, 1966, p. 108.

[27] R. E. Mapes *et al.*, 'School-Leavers' Hopes', *New Society*, Jan. 6, 1966.

[28] G. B. Hill, 'Choice of Career by Grammar School Boys', *Occupational Psychology*, Oct. 1965, p. 286.

[29] D. C. Beardslee and D. D. O'Dowd, 'Students and the Occupational World', in N. Sanford (ed.), *The American College*, New York: Wiley, 1962.

[30] A. Rodger and P. Cavanagh, 'Personnel Selection and Vocational Guidance', in A. Welford *et al.* (eds.), *Society: Problems and Methods of Study*, London: Routledge, 1962.

vocational guidance is given in schools than a few years ago, most youngsters are given little guidance before making their choice of an occupation. Very few secondary schools give curriculum time to careers choice. The Youth Employment Service offers, through the schools, information on available jobs and guidance to youngsters about the kind of work to which they may be suited. The service is not, however, widely used by school leavers, partly because it does not have the staff to reach more than a minority except on a group basis.

According to research by Sykes,[31] boys leaving school fall into three groups, determined by their home and school background plus their personality and ability: (1) those who know what kind of work they want to do and are keen to do it well, (2) those to whom work is something to be done as a matter of course, and to whom the job is not important provided that it offers some interest and fair conditions, and (3) the so-called problem cases—those who may easily drift into unsuitable occupations which will increase a tendency to instability or delinquency. Clearly, there is a need to extend vocational guidance back into the school as a form of educational case-work.

[31] E. G. Sykes, 'School and Work', *Sociological Review*, July 1953.

4

Industry and the Family

THE interaction between industry and the family is on two levels: relations between industrial organization and family structure as sub-systems of society and, on the role-person level, relations between the occupational and familial life-spheres of individuals. We first consider the influences which types of modern industrial organization have on the pattern of family life and the way in which occupational roles influence family roles. We then enquire to what extent family patterns exert pressures on various forms of industrial organization and behaviour, and how the individual's commitment to family life influences his performance in his job. Various types of relationship between work and family spheres of life are examined. Finally, we consider the special question of the increase in the proportion of married women who go out to work and the social prerequisites and consequences of this increase.

THE INFLUENCES OF INDUSTRY ON THE FAMILY

The influence of industry on family life may take a direct and an indirect form. In the direct form, the circumstances and attitudes associated with a certain kind of occupation affect circumstances and attitudes in the sphere of the family. In the indirect form, the association between occupation and family is mediated through social class, that is, being in an occupation is associated with being in a certain social class whose members, in turn, show characteristic behaviour patterns and attitudes. There is no rigid distinction between occupational influences and social class influences, and much of the empirical study of the relation between occupation and other spheres of social life rests upon 'social-class' data.[1] However, in considering the

[1] Cf. S. Nosow 'Social Correlates of Occupational Membership', in S. Nosow and W. H. Form (eds.), *Man, Work and Society*, New York: Basic Books, 1962.

influence of industry on the various aspects of family life the extent to which social class may also be a factor should be borne in mind.

Husband-Wife Roles

Industry, directly or indirectly, helps to shape the roles which are played within the family, as well as the relationships between these roles. In general, family and work spheres have become increasingly differentiated, due to the specialization of work roles in contemporary society.[2] However, when we look more closely at the degree of integration of work and family roles at various socio-economic levels we see particular differences.

At the upper levels of society, the role of the husband in the family may have little relationship to his role at work, and there may be little carry-over of the prestige and authority gained at work into family life. Work commitments tend to minimize the amount of time and energy which the husband can devote to his family, which becomes a subordinate part of his life. In the middle class, the financial standing and status of the family is more dependent on the occupation of the husband. But to the extent that he follows a technically complicated occupation which is incomprehensible to his family, his wife cannot identify strongly with his work. The middle-class husband's role in the family is not likely to be a dominant one, since the essential relationships in the family cluster around the mother and her children.

The working-class husband's occupation gives neither high income nor status in society at large. In communities where it is traditional for the husband only to work the separation of occupational and family life is almost complete. In working-class families where the wife also goes out to work, the additional income is often used to make the home a more comfortable place to stay in, and the husband's more dependent family role may approximate that of the middle-class husband.

The relation between work and family roles of husbands of two different occupational groups was compared by Gold and Slater.[3] They distinguished between the 'mass' family and the 'bureaucratic' family: the mass family is one in which the husband is either self-employed or working in a small organization, while the bureaucratic family has the husband working in a large organization. 'Mass' wives showed less power in family decision making, a higher evaluation of motherhood,

[2] R. and R. Rapoport, 'Work and Family in Contemporary Society', *American Sociological Review*, June 1965.

[3] M. Gold and C. Slater, 'Office, Factory, Store – and Family', *American Sociological Review*, Feb. 1958.

and a larger ideal family size. Another study by Blood and Wolfe characterized the main role of the wife in relation to her husband's occupation as collaborative, supportive or peripheral.[4] Farm wives much more often than urban wives collaborated with their husbands' jobs. The wives of white-collar workers most often thought they helped their husbands by giving encouragement, considerateness or entertainment (supportive), while the wives of blue-collar workers either contributed only housework or nothing (peripheral).

Kin Relationships

The network of relationship with members of the extended family shows the influence of occupation, both directly and indirectly. Bott's intensive study of a small number of English urban families suggests that ties among kin are likely to be stronger if they are able to help one another occupationally. In class terms, families with close-knit networks are likely to be working class, but not all working-class families have close-knit networks.[5] The strength of the family's neighbourhood network depends more directly on the husband's occupation within a given class. If he is engaged in an occupation in which his colleagues are also his neighbours, his network will tend to be localized. If he is in an occupation in which his colleagues are not his neighbours, his network will tend to become loose-knit.[6]

The influence of occupation on the family is seen also in the relationship of occupational mobility to the strength of extended family relations. According to Stuckert, there is an inverse relationship between mobility and contacts within the extended family.[7] However, a modified extended family can be consistent with occupational mobility. This extended family, by providing aid across class lines, permits the nuclear family to retain its extended family contacts despite differences in class position.[8]

Socialization

The father's experiences in the world of work are transmitted to the child both directly via occupation and indirectly via social class position. For some occupations the home may be the office or shop,

[4] R. O. Blood and D. M. Wolfe, *Husbands and Wives*, Glencoe: Free Press, 1960, p. 91.

[5] E. Bott, *Family and Social Network*, London: Tavistock, 1957, p. 221.

[6] *Ibid.*, p. 105.

[7] R. P. Stuckert, 'Occupational Mobility and Family Relationships', *Social Forces*, Mar. 1963.

[8] E. Litwak, 'Occupational Mobility and Extended Family Cohesion', *American Sociological Review*, Feb. 1960.

and the family will be aware of many of the father's job activities.[9] In some families the father will be very uncommunicative about his work, while in others the father may communicate virtually every detail of his work to his family. This is partly a matter of the types of personality involved, but is also related to the 'visibility' of the father's occupational role and the extent to which work is an integral part of life. Thus in farming households it is easy for children to start doing jobs around the farm without conceiving of these as 'work', and quite likely that they will also become farmers because the range of alternative occupations appears more restricted than to urban dwellers. By contrast, the technically complex and therefore less visible occupational role of many middle-class urban fathers means that they cannot serve as role models for their children.

The class position of the father has important influences on the socialization of the child.[10] At each level of society there tends to be a typical role pattern for children. Among upper-class families the care and raising of the child is often left in the hands of others besides the parents. The socialization of the child is directed at transmitting to him the values and norms of the upper classes. In the middle class, children and parents are much more directly concerned with each other. Socialization in the middle class aims to teach the child to behave 'properly', and more depends on the child's ability to compete successfully with others for the best education and hence for the best jobs. But in the working class the child is rarely driven to succeed or to live up to high standards of propriety; the emphasis is on obedience and keeping out of trouble.

Studies have been made seeking to test the influence of types of occupation on the severity or otherwise of socialization techniques. Research in Detroit reported by Miller and Swanson attempted to relate methods of child-rearing to the type of father's occupation.[11] Occupations were divided into those which demand initiative, individual action and risk taking (entrepreneurial) and those emphasizing conformity to established practices and the decisions of superiors (bureaucratic). The authors' hypothesis was that certain types of occupation attract certain types of husbands and wives and in turn create philosophies which are reflected in family behaviour. The hypothesis was borne out by results: 'entrepreneurial' parents were more

[9] W. G. Dyer, 'The Interlocking of Work and Family Social Systems Among Lower Occupational Families', *Social Forces*, May 1956.

[10] E. V. Schneider, *op. cit.*, pp. 444–46.

[11] D. R. Miller and G. E. Swanson, *The Changing American Parent*, New York: Wiley, 1958.

likely to train their children in self-control at an earlier age and in a greater number of respects than were 'bureaucratic' parents.

A further enquiry by McKinley considered the variables of autonomy, power and satisfaction in the work situation (within social class) in relation to socialization.[12] He found that more fathers in jobs low in autonomy used severe socialization techniques than did those in high autonomy positions. The same applied to those with no subordinates in the work situation compared with those with subordinates, and to those dissatisfied with their work compared with those satisfied. But the author warned against overlooking the problem of what kinds of personalities choose the different types of occupation, and stressed that more thorough study is needed before any conclusion can be made about causal processes.

THE INFLUENCE OF THE FAMILY ON INDUSTRY

Most available evidence points to the greater influence of industry on the family than vice versa, but it must not be supposed that family patterns and values have a negligible influence on industrialism or occupational life. As an example of the importance of the family structure in facilitating or hindering social change, Goode has compared the efforts of Japan and China to industrialize during the late nineteenth and early twentieth centuries.[13] Starting with similar social and economic conditions, Japan became far more industrially advanced than China during the early part of the twentieth century. Family differences between the two countries contributed to the difference in the rate of industrialization in several ways: the inheritance system in Japan made it easier to accumulate wealth for investment, nepotism was less a handicap than in China, and those who rose socially did not need to help the undeserving members of their families.

The present Japanese industrial system, despite being as technically advanced as that in many Western societies, provides an example of what Form and Miller call a 'family-mediated' type of industry-community relations.[14] The Japanese factory tends to be family-like in the roles and norms of its employees; employment is

[12] D. G. McKinley, *Social Class and Family Life*, New York: Free Press, 1964, Chap. 7.

[13] W. J. Goode, *The Family*, Englewood Cliffs: Prentice-Hall, 1964, pp. 114–16.

[14] W. H. Form and D. C. Miller, *Industry, Labor and Community*, New York: Harper, 1960, p. 394f.

normally for life, there is emphasis on intragroup harmony rather than on individual competition, and paternalistic care of the employee, even in his private life.[15] A similar pattern may be seen in Western industrial organizations where family values are dominant, often associated with family ownership of the enterprise or with religious or co-operative communities.

Family life is of concern to employers because a well-adjusted family member tends to be regular and punctual, better satisfied in his job, and a good teamworker.[16] Trade unions also generally approve a family system which produces loyal members, and this is especially so in the craft unions where the 'union ticket' is still often passed from father to son. A person's home life may affect job performance, and in large organizations there is sometimes a psychological consultant to smooth out home problems which may interfere with an employee's ability to work well.

TYPES OF WORK-FAMILY RELATION

We have seen that, at the institution-system level of analysis, the relation between industry and the family may vary between subordinating family life to the needs of industry to mediating purely industrial values with family values. To the extent that the structure and functioning of industrial organizations have a reciprocal relationship with the family life of employees, the analysis is also theoretically straightforward. At the role-person level, however, we need to look more closely at the factors influencing work and family interrelation to arrive at a theoretical framework into which research findings may be fitted.

As a starting point we may take one of the postulates of the Rapoports: work and family roles tend to be isomorphic (affecting each other in such a way as to induce *similar* structural patterns in both spheres) or heteromorphic (inducing different structural patterns).[17] Of the studies and observations which have been cited so far in this chapter, the family in which the wife collaborates with her husband in his work, the family whose home is the father's office or shop, the farming family, and to some extent the modern Japanese family, all exhibit isomorphism of work and family life, or an exten-

[15] J. C. Abegglen, *The Japanese Factory*, Glencoe: Free Press, 1958; K. Odaka, 'Traditionalism, Democracy in Japanese Industry', *Industrial Relations*, Oct. 1963.

[16] D. C. Miller and W. H. Form, *Industrial Sociology*, New York: Harper, 1964, p. 806.

[17] R. and R. Rapoport, *op. cit.*

sion of one sphere into the other. The other studies may be analysed into two further groups. If isomorphism represents a *positive* relationship between spheres, there is a *minimal* (approaching nil) relationship, as well as a *negative* relationship between them. A minimal relationship between work and family spheres is exemplified in families in which the husband's occupational role does not impinge on his family beyond affording it a certain style of life. Unlike the positive or negative patterns, the husband's occupational role has low visibility to his family. Occupations with regular hours, with no marked physical or psychological effects on the holder, and which do not encroach on his free time, are cases in point. Another way of putting this is to say that, in the life pattern as a whole, the relationship between work and family for these people is neutral rather than one of extension or opposition of spheres.

Having considered the patterns of extension and neutrality of spheres, we are left with the pattern of *opposition*. This pattern is seen in those manual occupations which generate in the husband a need for family life to function as compensation. Thus to repair the damages exacted by his work the miner tends to expect a wife who will feed and comfort him, making few demands in return.[18]

These three patterns of relationship between work and family spheres—extension, neutrality and opposition—are theoretically applicable to the relationship between other life-spheres. We shall return to this question in Chapter 14 when discussing the relationship between work and leisure. Meanwhile some of the features of these patterns, so far as work and family are concerned, may be set out as in Table 1.

The conclusions of some further research on work and family patterns may be fitted into this typology. A study by Podell showed that those who tended to be specific (orienting to others as means) or affectively neutral in their occupational role-expectations were more likely to view their occupational and familial lives as distinct and separate.[19] Those who were occupationally diffuse (responding to others as 'total persons') and affective were more prone to want their family included in their vocational world. These correspond to the neutrality and extension patterns respectively. The study by Aberle and Naegele of middle-class fathers' occupational role points to the element of opposition between work and family behaviour that

[18] S. Cotgrove and S. Parker, 'Work and Non-work', *New Society*, July 11, 1963.

[19] L. Podell, 'Sex and Role Conflict', *Journal of Marriage and the Family*, May 1966.

TABLE I

Type of relationship between spheres	*Extension* (positive)	*Neutrality* (minimal)	*Opposition* (negative)
type of occupation	farming, small shopkeeper, certain professional or craft ('mass')	technical, routine non-manual ('bureaucratic')	mining, fishing some 'impersonal' occupations
occupational characteristics	home and work location (partly) co-extensive	low visibility of occupation to family	physically or psychologically damaging work
husband's familial role in relation to occupational role	continuous with work	alternative to work	recuperation from work
role of wife in relation to husband's occupation	collaborative	supportive	peripheral

exists for those in some business occupations.[20] The business world limits responsibility and authority, judges people by what they can do rather than who they are, and often makes aggressiveness pay off—the opposite of which applies to successful family life.

Another example of opposition of spheres was revealed in the investigation by Dynes, who found that unsatisfactory interpersonal relationships in the family were significantly related to high occupational aspiration and satisfactory relationships to low occupational aspiration.[21] However, this probably reflects a culturally-based psychological need to succeed in at least one life sphere rather than a relationship between occupational or family life variables. Finally, research showing the extent to which members of certain occupations have their central life interest in the family sphere helps to test the hypothesis that impersonal occupations tend to lead to a higher affective investment in the family, and personal occupations to a lower investment in the family. Among a sample of bank employees, 35% gave family-oriented responses to a group of questions on central life interest,

[20] D. F. Aberle and K. D. Naegele, 'Middle-Class Fathers' Occupational Role and Attitudes Toward Children', in N. W. Bell and E. F. Vogel (eds.), *A Modern Introduction to the Family*, London: Routledge, 1961.

[21] R. R. Dynes *et al.*, 'Levels of Occupation Aspiration', *American Sociological Review*, April 1956.

among youth employment officers 25%, and among child care officers 19%—and these occupations are on a scale of decreasing impersonality.[22]

MARRIED WOMEN WORKING

Women constitute one-third of the labour force in Britain, and of these more than half are married. The proportion of all married women gainfully employed has risen steeply over the last few decades—it was 9% in 1921 against 21% in 1951 and 32% in 1961. The age group which has had the greatest increase in the 35–44 years. The children of these women have usually reached school age, thus affording the mothers more spare time in which to take up a job.

Conditions Making Increase Possible

The factors making an increase in the employment of married women possible may be considered under three heads: opportunity, capacity, and motivation.[23] Concerning *opportunity* there have been five main factors, the first three in relation to the industrial structure as a whole, and the other two being more specific to particular industries:

(1) *Shortage of labour*. During the last war it was necessary to recruit women to fill jobs left vacant by men in the forces, and many women stayed on in employment after the war. The manpower shortage was aggravated by a longer education and training period for juveniles and an increasing proportion of dependent old people to working population. Firms have been encouraged to establish branches in isolated areas to make use of possible reserves of married women.

(2) *Changes in the occupational structure*. The full employment policy has led to increased expenditure on consumer goods, thus expanding the retail trade which employs large numbers of women. Welfare and administrative workers for the social services, whose numbers have grown, are mainly women.[24]

(3) *Social disapproval weakened*. The presence of increasing numbers of single women in industry, greater equality in marriage, and the emancipation of women generally have resulted in the breaking down of traditions about a woman's place being in the home. However, these traditions persist in certain areas, for example, in mining communities.

[22] S. R. Parker, unpublished further analysis of a study reported in 'Work and Non-work in Three Occupations', *Sociological Review*, Mar. 1965.

[23] A. Myrdal and V. Klein, *Women's Two Roles*, London: Routledge, 1956.

[24] V. Klein, '*Britain's Married Women Workers*, London: Routledge, 1965, pp. 14–17.

(4) *Discrimination removed.* For example, the ban on married women teachers was lifted in 1944 and on married women in the metropolitan police force in 1946.

(5) *Changes in industry.* To encourage the employment of married women some factories have introduced special shifts allowing time for women to do their domestic duties. 'Controlled absence' has been accepted by some employers.[25] Training schemes have been developed to teach women new skills and techniques. With the introduction of new machines, manual work has become lighter and more amenable to women.

With regard to *capacity,* the health of the average working-class housewife has been improved with the benefits of the welfare state. 'The working-class housewife is not only freed from worry over immanent poverty, but her own health and strength have increased and she has the money and extra time to be freed from home duties, at least for short periods. Combined with a lower birthrate, these changes have greatly increased her capacity for employment.'[26] The middle-class housewife has generally had no experience of primary poverty which saps vitality and initiative. Labour-saving devices, by reducing the amount of work put into running the home, have helped to increase capacity for outside employment.

The *motivation* for married women to work has been the subject of several investigations.[27] The great majority of married women stressed that they had financial reasons for working, though in most cases this was to secure a higher standard of living generally or certain specific extras, such as children's education, rather than genuine economic necessity, which was claimed by a third or less of those interviewed. The desire to escape boredom and loneliness at home and to gain companionship at work has been shown to be an important additional motive, while for some, but relatively few working-class wives, the job itself is intrinsically interesting. Status striving is sometimes a motive, as when working-class families are transferred to new housing estates associated with status consciousness.

The findings concerning middle-class women's motives for working

[25] J. H. Smith, 'Managers and Married Women Workers', *British Journal of Sociology,* Mar. 1961; see also R. K. Brown *et al.*, 'The Employment of Married Women and the Supervisory Role', *British Journal of Industrial Relations,* Mar. 1964.

[26] L. Davidoff, *The Employment of Married Women in England 1850–1950,* Univ. of London M.A. thesis, 1956.

[27] V. Klein, *op. cit.*, pp. 36–44; R. K. Brown *et al.*, *op. cit.*, pp. 33–34; P. Jephcott *et al.*, *Married Women Working,* London: Allen and Unwin, 1962, pp. 87–88, 99–111.

have been similar. Financial considerations and relief from domestic tedium rank highest, with about equal frequency.[28] The increased cost of living and heavy taxation have in some cases made it necessary for wives to supplement the family income to keep up standards. Non-financial motives include the need for company and the desire to practise certain skills, especially when the women have had pre-marriage experience of interesting jobs with social contacts.

It is possible to analyse the various motives for married women to work according to the typology of relations between work and family spheres outlined earlier. Non-financial motives such as the intrinsic satisfaction derived from work or the desire to practise skills would be associated with the extension pattern. The need for company or for pocket money for extras would indicate a middling pattern of neutrality. But the motives of economic necessity or of desire to gain relief from domestic tedium show a strong element of opposition.

Effects in Work Sphere

The employment of part-time women workers involves more work in other respects, for example, extra staff may be needed in personnel, wages and medical departments of firms. Absenteeism is greater among women workers, making supervision and production planning more difficult. There is a greater tendency for working women to leave their jobs, but the study by Jephcott *et al.* of a Bermondsey factory revealed that women left their work not because of domestic duties but because of improved opportunities elsewhere.[29] Part-timers who stayed at least six months were likely to achieve a longer service with the company than full-timers.

Seear *et al.* investigated the careers of women in industry, particularly women scientists. 'Both the employers and the women agreed that the tendency for women to leave after a short period of employment was a serious obstacle to advancement. There was in fact both a shortage of women scientists for the jobs available and, at the same time, a shortage of supply of the jobs at the level and with the prospects women scientists sought.[30] Even where women were employed in responsible posts these were usually in research, advisory and specialist roles, and very few were in positions of line management, even at a low level in the line. It seems clear that the country is failing to make the best possible use of the abilities of women.

[28] M. Jefferys, *Mobility in the Labour Market*, London: Routledge, 1954.
[29] P. Jephcott *et al.*, *op. cit.*
[30] N. Seear *et al.*, *A Career for Women in Industry?*, Edinburgh: Oliver and Boyd, 1964.

Effects in Family Sphere

Wives who earn money by going out to work are more economically independent of their husbands than non-working wives. The division of labour for household chores is also changed, because the working wife has only about the same amount of free time as her husband (although there is an intermediate possibility of part-time work for the wife, particularly when there are small children). Greater equality in the occupational sphere between husbands and wives also seems to lead to greater equality in family decision-making. Thus Heer found that in Irish families, both in the working class and in the middle class, the working wife exerts more influence in family decision-making than the non-working wife.[31]

[31] D. M. Heer, 'Dominance and the Working Wife', *Social Forces*, May 1958.

5

Industry and Social Stratification

SOCIAL stratification means the division of members of a society into levels or strata which are united by some common attribute or characteristic.[1] Stratification is not a sub-system of society in the same sense as the economy, education or the family system; rather, it is a generalized aspect of the structure of all complex social systems. Nevertheless, it is possible to examine the relationship between social stratification as it is manifest in the sphere of industry and in the wider community. As we have seen with previous inter-institutional relationships, the process is reciprocal.

THE INFLUENCE OF INDUSTRY ON THE STRATIFICATION SYSTEM

Social stratification in modern industrial societies takes two major forms: class and status. Other forms of stratification, such as estates and castes, are not applicable. There is a large and controversial literature on problems associated with social classes,[2] but it is sufficient here to note the basic difference between the concepts of class and status. 'Class' is used to denote divisions of people according to their economic position in society, whether they are conscious of that position or not. Social status represents not a division of society but rather a gradation of positions determined by a variety of factors including, but not limited to, economic ones. Historically the concept of class was an important feature of Karl Marx's class theory of society, laying emphasis on successive class struggles between owners

[1] E. V. Schneider, *Industrial Sociology*, New York: McGraw-Hill, 1957 p. 373.

[2] A useful review is contained in T. B. Bottomore's *Classes in Modern Society*, London: Allen and Unwin, 1965; see also K. Prandy, *Professional Employees*, London: Faber and Faber, 1965, esp. Chap. 2.

and non-owners of the means of production, while Max Weber drew attention to another type of stratification deriving from the recognition of status which may cut across class structure.

The influence of industry on the stratification system in the wider society is most clearly seen in the phenomenon of social classes. Marxists believe that modern industrial societies are divided into two major social classes according to ownership or non-ownership of capital or property. Others who accept that there is a class division in society treat it more widely as a division between those with and without power, irrespective of whether that power is economic or not.[3] In the latter case it then becomes a matter of contention whether the non-economic power is in fact associated with economic position, that is, to what extent there is a generalized elite in society which has superior power or authority (legitimated power) in all social spheres.

The link between industry and stratification by status is weaker, mainly because of the wider range of bases for imputing status. If status situation is determined by a specific, positive or negative, social estimation of honour,[4] then it is clear that factors beyond economic and non-economic power and authority can be used to define status—such factors as consumption of goods, education, family background, and so on. However, this does not mean that no connection can be traced between such bases for ascribing status and economic position itself. As in the case of the influence of industry on the family, its influence on the stratification system may be a direct one via economic power and authority position in industry, or an indirect one via the spillover of status in industry into status in the community and the link between market situation and life style.

In Britain official statistics published by the Registrar-General describe 'social class' and 'socio-economic group' in terms of occupation. Non-academic research bodies often use an economic classification which is likely to identify life-style rather than occupation,[5] although it must be remembered that income is largely based on occupation. A survey by Kahan *et al.* showed that, when a sample of the British public was asked what sort of people it regarded as belonging to the middle and working classes, 61% gave occupational charac-

[3] E.g. R. Dahrendorf, *Class and Class Conflict in Industrial Society*, London: Routledge, 1959.

[4] H. H. Gerth and C. W. Mills, *From Max Weber*, London: Routledge, 1948, p. 187.

[5] E.g. the Hulton Readership Survey, which identified five classes ranging from the 'well-to-do' to 'the poor' (D. C. Marsh, *The Changing Social Structure of England and Wales 1871–1951*, London: Routledge, 1965, pp. 203-5).

teristics for the middle class and 74% for the working class.[6] A number of studies both in Britain and America indicate that people tend to put themselves in a higher (or sometimes lower) social class as compared with the official rating of their occupation or with the assessment of an interviewer.[7] These subjective judgments reflect a desire on the part of some individuals to identify with a stratum in society other than that in which their occupational membership puts them.

Three recent studies throw light on the factors which lead some people to emphasize their class position and others their status. Lockwood's account of *The Blackcoated Worker* shows that although the clerk is, in class terms, 'proletarian', he usually identifies himself in the middle class.[8] It is the work situation of the clerk, rather than his market-determined income, which gives the clue to his 'class-consciousness' and his negative attitude towards unionization. A later article by Goldthorpe and Lockwood examines the phenomenon of 'working-class affluence'.[9] By separating out the economic, relational and normative aspects of changes in working-class life, they conclude that, despite the economic progress of the working class in relation to the middle class, the gulf between the two remains very wide. Finally, Prandy concludes from his study of scientists and engineers that those who are in positions of authority tend to accept the 'status' view of stratification that they are part of a graded hierarchy, while those who do not share in the exercise of authority tend to have attitudes of a more class type.[10]

Studies of Occupational Status

As we have seen, stratification by social class is based on objective economic position, while stratification by status is concerned with finer and sometimes non-economic gradations. The question whether

[6] M. Kahan, D. Butler and D. Stokes, 'On the Analytical Division of Social Class', *British Journal of Sociology*, June 1966.

[7] British enquiries include a poll by the British Institute of Public Opinion showing that 47% of a sample of the general population assigned themselves to 'the middle classes' (G. D. H. Cole, *Studies in Class Structure*, London: Routledge 1955, p. 79); and a survey in two constituencies in which one-third of those classified as middle class by occupation identified themselves with the working class, while one-quarter of the manual workers considered themselves to be middle class (F. M. Martin in D. V. Glass (ed.), *Social Mobility in Britain*, London: Routledge, 1954, p. 57).

[8] D. Lockwood, *The Blackcoated Worker*, London: Allen and Unwin, 1958.

[9] J. H. Goldthorpe and D. Lockwood 'Affluence and the British Class Structure', *Sociological Review*, July 1963.

[10] K. Prandy, *op. cit.*

those individuals objectively assigned by occupation or economic position to a certain class agree with that placement has led to the term 'false class consciousness' being used to describe those who identify with the 'wrong' class. With status stratification, however, the whole matter is far more open. A great number of studies have been concerned with the differential statuses which occupations are thought to have. Some of these studies are described as of occupational 'prestige', but it seems better to use 'status' to refer to a position within a group or society and reserve 'prestige' for something more personal which an individual brings to a status.

Probably the best known British study of the social grading of occupations is the one by Hall and Jones.[11] They asked 1,400 people to rank thirty occupations in order of social grading, that is, they asked for their informants' views of what they thought was the general opinion. They concluded that there was no major difference in regard to the grading of selected occupations. The difference in average judgment was likely to be greater in grading occupations in the central region of the occupational scale than at the top or bottom, and there was a tendency for judgments about the social status of selected occupations to become more variable with the lower occupational status of informants.

Young and Willmott confirmed this last point in their study of the social grading of occupations by manual workers.[12] They found a considerable measure of dissensus among these workers, who tended to grade occupations according to their usefulness to society, putting manual workers above non-manual. The authors commented that 'in future enquiries it would be as well to ask people not only for their view of the general opinion about the standing of jobs but also for their own personal opinion.' These studies serve to underline the difference between the objective standing of an occupation and the respect accorded to it. The former relates to such dimensions as amount of earnings, education or qualifications needed; the latter relates to perception of functional necessity or social usefulness.

Criticism of Studies

Studies of the social grading of occupations may be objected to on the grounds that they force people into making distinctions which they do not normally make. The idea behind most occupational status

[11] J. Hall and D. Jones, 'Social Grading of Occupations', *British Journal of Sociology*, March 1950.

[12] M. Young and P. Willmott, 'Social Grading by Manual Workers', *British Journal of Sociology*, Dec. 1956.

studies is that occupations are scalable, that is, they can be located on a single scale of high to low according to their status. But, as Reiss points out, 'occupational rankings derived from the rating procedure . . . do not yield a unidimensional scale for all occupations . . . there are good reasons for assuming that status is a multidimensional phenomenon and that there is more than a single dimension to most of the conventional indicators of status.'[13]

One reason for the lack of universal agreement about the status of occupations may be that status is only one way of classifying occupations—the vertical way. Morris and Murphy have suggested the term 'situs' to describe a more horizontal classification by equally valued functional categories.[14] The use of the situs dimension provides us with a technique to assess the relative effect of *type* of work, as well as of class or status, on attitudes and behaviour.

Status Congruency

Differences in judgments of status may be partly explained by analysing the different sources of status. A job can carry status because of the rewards (economic or psychological) attached to it, because of prestige, authority, or functional importance.[15] These four sources of status may be congruous or not. If someone is high on status in one respect he will tend to feel relative deprivation if he is low on status in other respects. This leads to a 'strain towards congruency' of status attributes. This also operates on the group level—if one job is better than another by most values of a group there will be efforts by the generally higher-ranking group to bring all the status factors into line.[16]

There is the wider question of the extent to which status differences in the work milieu carry over into non-work life. A job with high status can help the entry into such things as golf clubs or fraternal associations. The motivation for some non-work activities involving positions of status, for example, in religious life or local government, may be the seeking of compensation for lack of status in occupational life.

[13] A. J. Reiss, *Occupations and Social Status*, Glencoe: Free Press, 1961.

[14] R. T. Morris and R. J. Murphy, 'The Situs Dimension in Occupational Stratification', *American Sociological Review*, April 1959.

[15] R. J. Pellegrin and F. L. Bates, 'Congruity and Incongruity of Status Attributes Within Occupations and Work Positions', *Social Forces*, Oct. 1959.

[16] G. C. Homans, *Sentiments and Activities*, London: Routledge, 1962, p. 93f.

THE INFLUENCE OF THE STRATIFICATION SYSTEM ON INDUSTRY

Industrial enterprises, collectively or individually, have a system of stratification which has internal and external aspects. Internally, the division of various types of workers and managers into strata may be held to be functional or dysfunctional for the enterprise or the industrial system as a whole. Externally, it is possible to trace the ways in which status stratification in the community influences the status privileges which are accorded to certain individuals in their occupational roles. These two aspects are analytically distinct, but in practice merge; as Bergel puts it, every stratification system finally correlates status and occupation.[17]

Just as there are social classes or status groups in society at large, so within industrial enterprises there are hierarchical levels of authority to which varying degrees of status are attached. Leaving aside the role of shareholders in providing capital for some types of industrial enterprise, the various roles in industry are structured by levels of authority, with the chief executive at the top and the ordinary workers at the bottom. The most common levels in this structure of 'line management' are outlined in Chapter 8. The point here is to examine the reasons for the existence of a stratification system in industry.

Those who hold a functionalist view of social organization seek to show that stratification is a necessary feature of any social order. Thus Davis and Moore argue that societies must provide rewards in order to induce individuals to fill the positions required by society.[18] Rewards must be distributed unequally to the various positions because those positions are not equally pleasant nor equally demanding in the training required. They conclude that the rewards and distribution become part of the social order and thus give rise to stratification. Barber points to the integrative function of stratification, though he maintains that it has both functional and dysfunctional relations with other parts of society and that it is the source of conflict as well as harmony.[19]

Tumin has criticized the basic premises of the Davis-Moore theory, especially the assumption that stratification is an inevitable feature of social organization.[20] Some of Tumin's counter-arguments are (1) It

[17] E. E. Bergel, *Social Stratification*, New York: McGraw-Hill, 1962, p. 330.

[18] K. Davis and W. Moore, 'Some Principles of Stratification', *American Sociological Review*, April 1945.

[19] B. Barber, *Social Stratification*, New York: Harcourt Brace, 1957, pp. 7, 11.

[20] M. Tumin, 'Some Principles of Stratification: A Critical Analysis', *American Sociological Review*, Aug. 1953.

cannot be demonstrated that it is unavoidable that differential prestige and esteem shall accrue to positions which command differential rewards in power and property, (2) Social stratification systems function to limit the possibility of discovering the full range of talent available in a society, and (3) They also function to encourage hostility, suspicion and distrust and thus to limit the possibilities of extensive social integration. Buckley also takes Davis and Barber to task for ignoring the distinction between stratification and differentiation, and holds that a classless society (containing no intergenerationally continuous strata) would differentiate its members in terms of duties, rights and perquisites and might recognize differential evaluation of roles.[21]

This debate concerning the necessity of stratification in society may be focussed on the narrower question of stratification in industry. Defenders of the status system in industry stress the need to recruit managers and technical experts by offering appropriate rewards, including those of high status. Critics of status consciousness in industry point to its divisive consequences, such as failure of communication between strata and (in class terms) the attitudes associated with the 'two sides of industry', i.e. management and workers.

There is ample evidence of the concern with status in industry on the part of both management and workers. Many managers expect their hours of work and privileges associated with their employment to be sharply distinguished from those of lower grades. A process of social differentiation is often active within a management structure as well as between managers and other employees. Clements, for example, found that senior management positions tended to be filled by men who were of higher social origin and who were even trained for senior management posts at an early point in their careers.[22]

Workers show concern for status in different ways. Those who are moved to another job at the same pay but with lower informal status often become deeply resentful.[23] Differences in wage rates between various jobs are also important in establishing status. Workers are usually more concerned with how their wages compare with others (the 'differential') than with absolute amounts—hence the difficulty of devising a generally acceptable wages policy. The difference be-

[21] W. Buckley, 'Social Stratification and the Functional Theory of Social Differentiation', *American Sociological Review*, Aug. 1958.

[22] R. V. Clements, *Managers: A Study of their Careers in Industry*, London: Allen and Unwin, 1958, p. 95.

[23] J. A. C. Brown, *The Social Psychology of Industry*, Harmondsworth, Pelican, 1954, p. 140.

tween shop floor and staff status can be a source of discontent; a recent survey of apprentices showed that those who were in an intermediate position between being close to staff status and far removed from it were most likely to be irritated by differences in treatment between staff and shop floor workers.[24]

There remains the question of to what extent status position in industry can be kept separate from status position outside industry. Part of the thesis of the *embourgeoisement* of the working class is that increasing numbers of its members adopt middle-class standards and patterns of life. Although this thesis can be accepted only with considerable qualification, it seems clear that some separation between status at work and status in the community has been effected. The principal factors in this process are the decreasing physical strain at work, shorter working hours, and the tendency to have central life interest in non-work spheres. Divorce between status at work and in the community is more possible in urban than rural areas, because status is ascribed to categories who share clusters of characteristics but with whose component members one does not necessarily interact.[25] The fact that the consumption standards (an obvious 'status attribute') of the working class have become more like those of the middle class cannot be denied, even though social strata within industry and the authority relationships on which they are based have remained broadly unchanged.

[24] T. S. Chivers and S. R. Parker, 'The Apprentice Technician and His Job', *Industrial Society*, Oct. 1966.

[25] R. Frankenberg, *Communities in Britain*, Harmondsworth, Pelican, 1966, p. 263.

6

Industry, the Community and the Polity

In this final chapter in the section dealing with the relation between industry and other sub-systems of society, we shall consider under the broad heading of 'the community and the polity' some of those aspects of society not covered in previous chapters. By the community is meant a continuous geographical area in which mutually dependent groups act together to satisfy their needs through a common set of organizations and institutions.[1] By the polity is meant the sub-system of society oriented to the generation and allocation of power, the relation of the polity and government being conceived as approximately parallel to that of the economy and business.[2]

INDUSTRY AND THE COMMUNITY

Industry Influences the Community

Industry, in the broad sense of technology, economic enterprises and persons associated with these, has pervasive effects on the communities which it serves and from which it draws its resources. These effects may be considered under three heads: values, the physical effects on the community, and the purposive attempts of industrial interest groups to influence society.

Industry feeds into the community people whose personalities reflect their experiences at work. Just as Weber showed that, in addition to technical possibilities and material conditions, the appropriate values were necessary to the development and maintenance of traditional capitalist society, so a certain set of basic minimum values are

[1] W. A. Anderson and F. B. Parker, *Society: Its Organization and Operation*, New Jersey: Van Nostrand, 1964, p. 102.

[2] Talcott Parsons, *Structure and Process in Modern Societies*, Glencoe: Free Press, 1960, p. 42.

necessary to the maintenance of modern capitalism. People generally must accept their position both in the industrial structure and in the wider social structure. Because production is dependent on consumption, they must be persuaded to want the goods and services which industry is capable of producing—industry is given the function both of making the goods and of making the desires for them.[3] This involves values at the 'macro' level of society, but there are also more local and specific changes in values brought about by changes in industry. For example, the effect on Oxford of the growth of the motor-car industry may be cited: its change to a high-wage town led to alterations in old-established ideas about the informal hierarchy of jobs amongst the wage-earners.[4]

Industry has certain physical effects on the communities in which it operates. In various ways the community feels the effect of what is happening in industry. Where towns are heavily dependent on a single industry, the fortunes of that industry will determine whether the town prospers or declines. The establishment of new industries in an area will affect the total number and spatial distribution of workers. To take the South Wales industrial area as an example, new employment regions have taken over from the small, relatively independent mining and tinplate towns.[5] These new regions tend to have new centres of employment, between which are areas of comparative industrial stagnation from which work forces for the new centres are drawn.

The purposive attempts of industrial interest groups to influence society may be seen in their efforts to make a favourable impression on public opinion. Advertising, in addition to its manifest function of promoting the products of the firm, has also the latent function of promoting the firm itself, a function which is more specifically performed by public relations departments. Many large firms organize parties of visitors to tour their works. On the side of labour, the 'public relations' activities of trade unions are generally less in evidence. Trade union leaders appear on television to put their case in disputes with employers, but union journals are circulated mainly amongst union members.

Another, and more theoretical, way of looking at the mutual influences of industry and the community is to identify types of industry-community relations. Although there are separate economic interest

[3] J. K. Galbraith, *The Affluent Society*, London: Hamish Hamilton, 1958, p. 122.

[4] J. M. Mogey, *Family and Neighbourhood*, Oxford: University Press, 1956, p. 5.

[5] G. F. Thomason, paper read to Town Planning Conference, Cardiff, 1966.

groups within industry such as those of commerce, industry, agriculture, finance, and organized labour, for some purposes most of these groups (excluding labour) may be regarded as one wider interest group which interacts with the community. Form and Miller have suggested that there are five types of relationship between this wide economic interest group and the community.[6]

(1) *business-dictated* is where employers dictate working hours without much concern for their effect on home life, and workers must accommodate their family life to industrial operations (this is likely in a one-industry town with a limited labour market or an industry-dominated town with weak or no organized labour),

(2) *business-dominated* is similar to the above, but management works out certain conditions of work with the union, while retaining work rules and hours as a management prerogative (likely where management authority is strong, also a fairly strong union, with some surplus labour),

(3) *labour-mediated*: unions attempt to share management's right to determine working hours, and there may be labour-management councils (strong labour union, industry dependent on local skilled labour),

(4) *equilibrium*: unions are strong, and so are other community influences, for example, civic associations; management decisions have to be considered in the light of their effect on the local community (highly integrated community), and

(5) *family-mediated*: family values are dominant (family ownership of the enterprise, religious or co-operative communities).

These types of relationship between industry and community have been worked out in connection with American industrial and social conditions and need to be modified if applied to Britain. Thus the business-dictated pattern would be hard to find in Britain, except in the sense that certain types of both manual and non-manual workers are motivated by high pay or a sense of vocation to subordinate their family and leisure lives to the demands of the work.[7] The authors also suggest that there are four approaches to industry-community relations[8]: (1) *structural-functional,* involving social ramifications of industry into other sub-systems, (2) *compensation,* in which industry is seen as a source of community satisfaction denied in the local

[6] W. H. Form and D. C. Miller, *Industry, Labor and Community,* New York: Harper, 1960.

[7] Examples of manual workers in these circumstances are those engaged in oil drilling, tunnelling or distant-water fishing, and of non-manual workers, some business executives, social work or medical personnel.

[8] *Op. cit.*, p. 644f.

community,[9] (3) the *welfare* approach to community structure, industry taking part as a responsible partner, and (4) *power*, industry being the major source of power affecting the community.

The Community Influences Industry

The above theoretical approaches to industry-community relations may be illustrated by examples of ways in which community norms and values exert influence on industrial structure and behaviour. Deferring consideration of the more political influences until the next section, we may concentrate on cases in which management has to adjust its practices to the social and cultural realities of communities in which it operates. The processes of adjustment between the circumstances and attitudes of the mass of workers and the behaviour which management requires of them are not easy to trace, although the extent to which one side accommodates to the other is a function of the power relations existing between them. Adjustment on the side of industry (represented by management) may be seen most clearly in the cases of minority groups of employees, of which juveniles, women and immigrant workers may be taken as examples.

As we saw in Chapter 3, there are various ways in which management accepts the fact that some juvenile workers need to complete their education by taking part in day-release, sandwich and other training courses. The community's idea of appropriate education takes precedence over at least some employers' aim of maximizing profits from employing juvenile labour. In the case of women workers, many factory managers have found it necessary to make special arrangements concerning shifts and to accept 'controlled absenteeism' when the women want time off to look after their domestic duties.[10]

The employment of immigrant workers, particularly coloured workers, poses a different kind of problem for industry. The degree of integration of coloured workers into the labour force is part of the wider issue of the integration of coloured citizens into the community at large. This means that some employers are conscious of a conflict between the policies they feel they have to pursue as employers and those which, as citizens, they feel they would like to see followed.[11] Sometimes they will set out reasons showing how it is uneconomic

[9] This view was put forward by Elton Mayo (*The Social Problems of an Industrial Civilization*, Harvard: University Press, 1945) to stress the importance of group life in industry.

[10] J. H. Smith, 'Managers and Married Women Workers', *British Journal of Sociology*, March 1961.

[11] M. Banton, *The Coloured Quarter*, London: Cape, 1955, p. 148.

for them to employ coloured labour when whites are available, but are uncomfortable about the implications of this if all employers were to do the same.

In various ways the community feels the effect of events and changes that take place in industry. Labour-management relations are usually felt to be the internal concern of industry and government, but when strikes, lockouts or redundancies occur a wider public is interested because of the plight of unemployed workers and the effect on the economic well-being of the community. On the national level the wages and salaries paid to employees and the prices charged to consumers for goods and services have become of interest to those other than persons directly affected, because of the movement towards centralized control of prices and incomes. On the role-person level, the social life of employees has a bearing upon industrial organization, efficiency and morale. It is now a commonplace of industrial sociology that attitudes and behaviour in industry—such as absenteeism, labour turnover, pressures for minimum or maximum effort—cannot be explained by reference to conditions in industry alone, but are also dependent on norms, values, roles, expectations and statuses in non-industrial spheres.

INDUSTRY AND THE POLITY

Industry and Political Influence

Industry operates in a societal environment and has certain relations of power with that environment. Power is generated and exercised within industrial organizations and also outside these, the latter area being our chief concern here. The forms of influence which industry has in the political sphere may be divided into the direct and the indirect, or perhaps more precisely into organized group and dual-role individual. In seeking to influence central and local government policies, representatives of industrial interests may form themselves into organized pressure groups, while the personnel of industrial undertakings may also have part-time political roles through which their economic interests may be promoted.

Pressure groups are part of the modern political scene: they have been defined as organized groups possessing both formal structure and real common interests, in so far as they seek to influence the process of government.[12] One of the major forms of pressure groups is the economic, including employers, manufacturers and traders on the

[12] J. D. Stewart, *British Pressure Groups*, Oxford: Clarendon Press, 1958, p. 1.

one hand and organized labour (trade unions and professional associations) on the other. Although in recent years the Labour party has extended its appeal to groups on its right and the Conservative party its appeal to groups on its left, each has core support from the trade union movement in the one case and business interests in the other. These pressure groups operate through processes of consultation and advice. Some references to consultation occur in statutes but mostly it has little formal expression in the outward structure of government except by means of advisory committees. In addition, the general strategy of pressure groups in seeking to influence decision-making bodies is carried out through tactics of influencing public opinion by petition, advertising, public meeting, the activities of individual M.Ps. and those of lobbyists.

The ability of members of industry (usually management members) to influence political policies by direct participation in government is an aspect of control by interlocking elites in industry and government which was referred to in Chapter 2. Retired ministers in Conservative governments often, and in Labour governments occasionally, take seats on the boards of top industrial companies and banks.[13] The interlocking of industrial and government control was at its peak in wartime when leading industrialists moved into government posts to operate wartime controls, but in the post-war period the nationalized industries have provided many opportunities for top appointments of industrialists and trade union leaders. At the level of local government, it is significant that employers, managers and professional people are over-represented four times on local councils in proportion to their numbers in the general population.[14] It is not suggested that there is normally anything improper in combining the roles of businessman and councillor, although occasionally individuals are accused of taking advantage of their public office for personal gain.

Political and Legal Constraints on Industry

Most of the relationships between industry and other sub-systems of society which we have considered in previous chapters and in the first part of this chapter have shown industry to have a greater effect on other sub-systems than vice versa. In the case of the political-legal sphere this is not so. Although the *degree* of control of industry

[13] M. Barratt Brown, 'The Controllers', *Universities and Left Review*, Autumn 1958.

[14] L. Moss and S. R. Parker, *The Local Government Councillor*, London, HMSO 1967.

deemed desirable has been hotly debated, there is today no question that *some* controls are necessary to maintain economic and social stability and ensure the rough compatibility of economic and other social interests. Legal regulation of industry has been clearly established but there is still controversy as to how far it should go.

The role of the government (or more broadly of the state) in industry may be considered under a number of headings: as controller, regulator, promoter, entrepreneur, and planner.[15] The state has acquired economic functions in a haphazard and piecemeal fashion, and so it is hardly surprising that these are exercised by many different bodies: central departments (mainly the Board of Trade and the Ministry of Labour), local authorities, a variety of independent public boards, commissions and corporations, and even private bodies that have been specially endowed with public powers. The ways in which direct governmental control of industry is exercised include budgetary policy, discriminatory taxation, hire-purchase controls, the control of public investment and of the distribution of industry.

In its role as regulator the state provides a framework for the orderly operation of business enterprise. Some of the main ways in which it does this are by incorporation of companies, registration of trade unions and employers' associations, various measures for the protection of the consumer and the investor, control of restrictive trading agreements and of wages and conditions of work. The state also attempts to sponsor and promote the interests of industry in various ways. It promotes industrial and agricultural research, and is interested in improving industrial productivity and efficiency. Public ownership and regulation plays a part in industrial reconstruction, and there is regulated marketing of staple agricultural and some horticultural products and of fish through marketing boards. Other measures of direct support for trade include tariffs and other protection for domestic industries and the promotion of exports. The government is also interested in improving industrial relations and provides employment services, industrial training and technical education.

In its role as entrepreneur the state directly participates in the economy in four ways. It is an important purchaser of goods and services for its own use; it is a large employer (about one million out of a working population of twenty-five millions); it exercises a considerable direct influence on employment in other parts of the public services which it finances and supervises but does not manage;

[15] These roles correspond to chapter headings in J. W. Grove's *Government and Industry in Britain* (London: Longmans, 1962), where these matters are discussed in detail.

and it produces and trades on a limited scale for its own use. Finally, as planner the government extends its role as controller. The machinery for directing and guiding the economy has traditionally been highly decentralized but recent events, such as the establishment of the National Economic Development Council and the Prices and Incomes Board, indicate that the economic difficulties facing the country are likely to produce revolutionary changes in the relation between industry and the government.

Industrial Relations and the Law

The piecemeal and somewhat reluctant intervention of the state in the affairs of industry is paralleled by a similar piecemeal and reluctant intervention of the law in the field of industrial relations. As Wedderburn remarks, the law tends to make its appearance only when things go radically wrong.[16] The reasons for this must be sought in the forms in which collective bargaining between employers and unions has developed in this country and in the history of trade unionism. Collective bargaining has been essentially voluntary and is today covered by very few decisions of the judges because it has rarely been brought into any court. In the nineteenth and early twentieth centuries legal intervention was inimical to the trade unions,[17] and the fact that greater legal control of unions and industrial relations is now a party political issue indicates that organized labour is still generally opposed to any increase in the role of the law.

Apart from the vexed question of industrial relations, there are two main areas which fall within the province of labour law. These are (1) the employment relationship between worker and employer, which still rests largely upon the common law governing the individual contract of employment, and (2) the statutory control of certain conditions of employment, especially the payment of wages and safety and similar conditions at work.

Occupation and Political Behaviour

It is possible to trace an association between type of occupation and voting behaviour or active political participation. The data again are mostly in terms of social class or socio-economic group. Of the working class about two-thirds usually vote Labour, and of the middle

[16] K. W. Wedderburn, *The Worker and the Law*, London: MacGibbon and Kee, 1966, p. 13.

[17] Evidence for this is given in *ibid.* p. 20f.

class 70-85% vote Conservative.[18] Although Labour party members are generally distributed occupationally in proportion to Labour voters, more Conservative party members come from non-manual groups in proportion to Conservative voters.[19] In both parties manual workers are not represented among the leaders in proportion to their numbers among the electors. An occupational analysis of the 1966 Parliament showed that whereas manual workers (about 67% of the working population) provided 30% of Labour M.Ps. they provided less than 1% of Conservative M.Ps.[20] Professional workers were heavily over-represented among M.Ps. of both parties.

Studies of particular localities and occupational groups supplement the findings on a national scale. In Derby it was found that there was very little difference between the political participation of non-manual and skilled manual workers, but unskilled manual workers participated less often.[21] It is reasonable to suppose that greater autonomy and participation in work decisions predisposes a worker to greater interest in political matters. Also, particular occupations seem to be associated with political militancy, such as car workers and dockers. The politically militant are not all lower paid workers, but may include those in occupations with a traditional 'radical ethos', notably the highly paid London compositors studied by Cannon.[22]

[18] M. Abrams, 'Class Distinction in Britain', in *The Future of the Welfare State*, London: Conservative Political Centre, 1958; see also J. Bonham, *The Middle-Class Vote*, London: Faber and Faber, 1954.

[19] J. Blondel, *Voters, Parties, and Leaders*, Harmondsworth: Pelican, 1963, p. 91.

[20] D. Butler and A. King, *The British General Election of* 1966, London: Macmillan, 1966.

[21] T. Cauter and J. Downham, *The Communication of Ideas*, London: Chatto and Windus, 1954.

[22] I. Cannon, *The Social Situation of the Skilled Worker*, Univ. of London PhD thesis, 1961.

7

Sociological Approaches to Organizations

ORGANIZATION analysis is one of the most significant areas of the middle-range level of theory to be developed in the last decade. The significance derives from three main developments: recognition that macro-sociological analysis and micro-sociological analysis are mediated by structures not adequately examined at either level; the expansion of interest in inter-organization and intra-organization variables as a basis for examining similarities and differences in work and non-work organizations; and the acceptance that formal and informal structures isolated by the classical and neo-classical schools of industrial sociology are not alternatives since the organization includes both, and is a partly open system. As the rest of the section is concerned with particular aspects of work organizations, the intention in this introductory chapter is to consider the scope and directions of inter-organization and intra-organization analysis and comparative organization theory.

Weber's formulations concerning the 'ideal type' of bureaucracy[1] have provided a basis for the contemporary reformulations in organization analysis, although much organization theory does not take its point of departure from Weber. His ideas have been criticized in two ways.[2] There are those who have examined organizations for their bureaucratic characteristics and created new 'ideal types' where organizations did not match Weber's formulation. This approach has been adopted

[1] For a treatment of rationality in Weber's analysis see T. Parsons' introduction to M. Weber, *The Theory of Social and Economic Organization*, New York: Oxford University Press, 1947; also R. Bendix, *Max Weber, An Intellectual Portrait*, London: Heinemann, 1960, pp. 284–5, footnotes.

[2] See D. S. Pugh *et al.*, 'A Conceptual Scheme for Organizational Analysis', *Administrative Science Quarterly*, March 1963, pp. 289–315.

by Gouldner, Crozier, Constas and Gerth.[3] The major concern has been with work organizations. The second approach has been to compare the organization's functioning with Weber's description of bureaucracy and to point out that his formulations were incomplete and inadequate. This approach has been adopted by Eisenstadt, Blau, Merton, Bendix and Udy.[4]

THE COMPARATIVE BASIS OF WORK ORGANIZATIONS

Attempts to move away from the bureaucracy-rationality problem and to outline a comparative basis for the formal structure of work organizations have received impetus from the inadequacies of Weber's formulation. The approaches of Burns and Stalker[5] and Pugh and Hickson[6] are the most significant contributions. Burns and Stalker have polarized work organizations on a mechanistic-organismic ideal type continuum whilst Pugh and Hickson have postulated an empirical approach to the dimensions of work organizations.

The work of Burns and Stalker derives partly from the studies by Marcson and Kornhauser of work organizations with dynamic technologies,[7] and partly from the stress by Woodward on the extent to which technology prescribes the authority structure of work organizations.[8] The central thesis is that not only have there been two distinct kinds of approaches to work organization analysis[9] but these represent two different sets of empirical circumstances. The *mechanistic* model is applicable to stable structures which rest on a predictable market and the hierarchic authority structure inherited

[3] These writers deserve separate treatment which cannot be given to them here.

[4] S. N. Eisenstadt, 'Bureaucracy and Bureaucratization', *Current Sociology, A Trend Report*, Vol. 7, 1958, pp. 99–164; P. M. Blau, *The Dynamics of Bureaucracy*, Chicago University Press, 1955; R. K. Merton, *Social Theory and Social Structure*, Glencoe: Free Press, 1957; R. N. Bendix 'Bureaucracy: The Problem and its Setting', *American Sociological Review*, 1947, pp. 493–507; S. H. Udy, 'Bureaucracy and Rationality in Weber's Organization Theory', *American Sociological Review*, Dec. 1959, pp. 791–95.

[5] T. Burns and G. M. Stalker, *The Management of Innovation*, London: Tavistock, 1961.

[6] D. S. Pugh *et al.*, *op. cit.*

[7] S. Marcson, *The Scientist in American Industry*, Princeton University, 1960; W. Kornhauser and W. O. Hagstrom, *Scientists in Industry*, Berkeley: California University Press, 1962.

[8] J. Woodward, *Management and Technology*, London: HMSO, 1958: and more recently *Industrial Organization*, London: Oxford University Press, 1965.

[9] For a summary of these two approaches see A. Etzioni (ed.), *Complex Organizations*, New York: Holt, Rinehart and Winston, 1961, pp. 18–47.

from the typical ownership pattern of early capitalism. This model is characterized internally by specialized work role differentiation, hierarchic control and communication, clear delimitation of tasks and a stress upon technical means rather than changing ends. When the technology becomes unstable and markets less predictable, however, the tendency is for the work organization to approach the *organismic* model with adjustment and continual redefinition of work roles, a network of control and communication and a stress upon the changing ends rather than stable means. Burns and Stalker point to various pathological consequences of the mechanistic type structure attempting to cope with the dynamic technology and diffuse authority of the organismic type. The importance of their analysis is that it moves away from the bureaucracy-rationality dispute and provides a basis for the comparative study of work organizations.

Pugh and Hickson have attempted to tackle the problem of the formal analysis of work organization by a factorial rather than process analysis.[10] Rejecting the idea that technology is the deciding factor in features of organizations and limiting attention to the objective structure, they distinguish four kinds of variables: activity, structural, contextual and performance. The *activity* variables are those delineated by Bakke,[11] namely identification, perpetuation, workflow control and homeostasis. The *structural* variables are six: specialization, standardization, formalization, centralization, configuration and flexibility. These structural dimensions are the most significant aspect of the analysis and thus they can be dealt with in a little more detail.

Specialization refers to the traditional concept of division of labour; this includes the number of specialisms, the degree of role specialization, the amount and kind of professionalization and relationship between 'technical complexity and the relative status and influence of particular specialisms'. Two aspects of standardization are dealt with: standardization of procedures and standardization of roles. The first, it is suggested, can be classified by adapting Bales'[12] interaction categories and is concerned with 'decision-seeking . . . decision-making, information conveying procedures and procedures for the operationalization or carrying-out of decisions'. Standardization of these proce-

[10] Factor analysis is a statistical method of treating variables without *a priori* assumptions about significance; process analysis is concerned with deductive definitions and relationships.

[11] E. W. Bakke, *Bonds of Organization*, New York: Harper, 1950.

[12] R. F. Bales, *Interaction Process Analysis, A Method for the Study of Small Groups*, Cambridge, Mass.: Addison-Wesley Press, 1951; also 'A Set of Categories for the Analysis of Small Group Interaction', *American Sociological Review*, Vol. 15. 1950, pp. 257–263.

dures is regarded as existing 'when there are rules or definitions that cover all circumstances or apply invariably'. The standardization of roles refers to how far the work organization 'prescribes the standardization of role definitions and qualifications for office, role performance measurement, titles for office... and rewards for role performance'. Formalization, as the third structural dimension, refers to the extent to which 'communications and procedures in an organization are written down and filed'.

Two of the last three structural dimensions refer to the classical work organization theorists' central focus, namely authority. Centralization and configuration are seen as distinct aspects of this variable; centralization 'concerns the locus of authority to make decisions affecting the organization' and includes such factors as 'the location of actual decision-making functions at particular points in the authority structure; the promulgation of rules for decisions which limit discretion of subordinates; the frequency and thoroughness of review procedures and control systems; the legitimate availability of relevant information'. Centralization initially requires establishment of the range and scope of the chief executive and then 'the range of levels down the organization to which the performance evaluations of the executive are applicable'. Configuration refers to the shape of the authority structure and particularly the vertical and lateral spans of control, criteria for departmental division, and the number of positions in the various divisions. The last dimension is that of flexibility and refers to the amount and speed of organization change.

Contextual variables, as the third major class of variables, are an attempt to take into account a variety of non-generalizing characteristics. Historical differences, different forms of ownership, variations in size, ideology, technology, location, resources and inter-dependence with other organizations, have been among those which have made deductive approaches inappropriate. Pugh and Hickson suggest that these contextual variables can be related to the structural variables by factor-analysis. The fourth kind of variable is *performance,* or simply, 'an organization's success in reaching its stated goals'.

Although the empirical study, of which the above is the theoretical framework, is still incomplete, the analysis is a considerable advance towards an objective theory of work organizations.

COMPARATIVE ORGANIZATION ANALYSIS

It is questionable whether either of the above approaches can provide a framework for a comparative analysis which includes both work and non-work organizations. This comparative framework has been attempted by functionalist theorists who have usually differentiated between the kinds of goals organizations as systems attempt to realize, and then have related goal differences to the wider institutional structure, or to internal structural differences in the organization; some have attempted both. Four theorists are considered as offering a comparative basis for work and non-work organizations; Blau and Scott,[13] Etzioni,[14] Parsons[15] and Argyris.[16]

Blau and Scott suggest that a fourfold classification according to the criteria of 'who benefits' is the most useful way of distinguishing types of organizations. Answering this question leads to differentiation of four basic categories of persons; the members or rank and file participants, the owners, the clients or 'public in contact', and the public at large. Four kinds of organization are identifiable with the four categories of persons: 'mutual benefit' organizations, 'business concerns', 'service organizations' and 'commonweal organizations'. This functional classification is used to look at kinds of problems typically related to each kind of organization. The basic problem of mutual benefit organizations is that of maintaining control over members; that of the business concern 'the achievement of maximum gain at minimum cost in order to further survival and growth in competition with other organizations'; service organizations have a distinct set of problems which cluster around the provision of professional services; whilst commonweal organizations have three problems, 'of power, of promoting extra-ordinary performances and . . . dealing with outcasts'.

Blau and Scott summarize a great deal of the ever growing body of literature surrounding organization theory, but it is doubtful whether their typology resolves some fundamental problems in the classification of organizations. This comment also applies to Etzioni.[17]

[13] P. Blau and W. R. Scott, *Formal Organizations*, London: Routledge 1963.

[14] A. Etzioni, *A Comparative Analysis of Complex Organizations*, New York: The Free Press of Glencoe, 1961.

[15] T. Parsons, 'Suggestions for a Sociological Approach to the Theory of Organizations', *Administrative Science Quarterly*, June 1956, pp. 63–85, and Sept. 1956, pp. 224–239; and also H. A. Landsberger, 'Parsons' Theory of Organizations' and W. F. Whyte, 'Parsonian Theory Applied to Organizations', both in M. Black (ed.) *The Social Theories of Talcott Parsons*, New York: Prentice-Hall, 1961; see also T. Parsons, *Structure and Process in Modern Societies*, Glencoe: Free Press, 1960, pp. 16–96.

[16] C. Argyris, *Integrating the Individual and the Organization*, New York: Wiley, 1964.

[17] It would appear that many of the insights of Etzioni, particularly the assertion of independent sources of instrumental involvement recently advanced

Etzioni bases his classification on the variable of *compliance*. Compliance is both an interactional and psychological variable; it is interactional in that it refers to 'a relation in which an actor (or role occupant) behaves in accordance with a directive supported by another actor's power'; it is psychological in that it refers to 'the orientation of the subordinated actor to the power applied'. Compliance, then, is the 'major element of the relationship between those who have power and those over whom they exercise it and is universal, existing in all social units.' In developing compliance as a basis for organization classification, Etzioni distinguishes three steps; a distinction between three kinds of power, a distinction between three kinds of involvement, and finally the association of kinds of power with kinds of involvement. It is 'these associations which are compliance relationships' and which 'serve as a basis for organization classification'.

The three kinds of power means are coercive, remunerative, and normative. Accepting that empirically all kinds of power may be present in the organization, Etzioni suggests that there will be a tendency towards type of power means to align with type of involvement. Involvement is the 'cathectic-evaluative orientation of an actor towards an object' and can differ in intensity and direction as well as kind. Differences in kind are three: alienative involvement, calculative involvement and moral involvement.

The third step in Etzioni's analysis is to relate types of power means to types of involvement. These two components constitute the compliance relationship by which types of organization are distinguished. Etzioni suggests that congruency will tend to be exhibited between coercive power and alienative involvement, remunerative power and calculative involvement, and normative power and moral involvement. This congruency tendency is seen as deriving from 'internal and external pressures on the organization to be effective'. Based on this typology of congruency, three major kinds of organization are classified. Those which use coercive power and tend to generate alienative involvement are 'total institutions' such as prisons. Those which use remunerative power and tend to generate calculative involvement are work organizations (although this applies mainly to manual workers). The third compliance relationship, between norma-

by J. Goldthorpe ('Attitudes and Behaviour of Car Assembly Workers: A Deviant Case and a Theoretical Critique', *British Journal of Sociology*, Sept. 1966) make such findings not unexpected. It is questionable whether this postulated independence takes the issue very much further however, since the problem is the one of interdependence.

tive power and moral involvement applies to 'at least nine frequently found types of normative organization'. These are, religious, ideological, general hospitals, universities, voluntary associations and (although less typical since they include some coercive element) schools, therapeutic mental hospitals, professional organizations and core organizations of social movements.

Thus far the assumption that there will be congruency between types of 'power means' used and the type of involvement, has been stated rather than explained. This tendency to congruency derives from the hypothesis that different kinds of organizations attempt to realize different kinds of goals. Etzioni rejects the establishment of formal goals deriving from the explicit statement of such goals by the organization or its top élite; instead he suggests that the essential distinction is between the goals which organizations attempt to realize. These are three: order goals, economic goals and culture goals. The tendency towards congruency thus derives from the effectiveness of the three types of compliance in relation to these three types of goals. Organization effectiveness in terms of the compliance-goal relationship may be impeded by any one of the three major variables making up the relationship: involvement, power, goals.

The three variables, as Etzioni recognizes, span the organization-role and role-person levels of analysis. In that both Blau and Scott and Etzioni take their point of departure from the problem of classifying organizations functionally they are similar. Neither offers, however, a means of moving from the organization level to the broader institution-system level, although both are extremely fruitful in raising the critical issues of power and involvement as central differences between organizations. It is suggested that many of the problems of concern in work organizations fall within Etzioni's classification, in that kinds of work involvement and how power means structure social relationships are the disputed issues. It can be contended that Etzioni does not fully treat the problem of technology, but he makes no assumptions about involvement, power or goals. The extent to which different kinds of involvement are conditioned by membership in other systems, previous value commitments[18] of participants and basic personality structure is left open for empirical investigation, as is the relationship between the different kinds of power which the organization can exercise and their dependency upon the resources it can command. Equally open to empirical investigation is the extent to which organization goals are circumscribed by the values of the social environment

[18] See Chapter 13.

in the sense of both the origin of goals and changes in goals which the organization can initiate.

Thus far attention has been on attempts to provide a basis for a comparative approach to work organizations by establishing the objective structure of such organizations or suggesting 'ideal types'. The second approach has been broader and suggested variables by which work and non-work organizations can be distinguished. This second approach has tended to a functional classification in terms of the goals which organizations seek to realize as well as how these affect the internal structure. There are two questions which arise from the approaches noted. Firstly, is the formal structure which the inductive-empirical approach attempts to quantify best thought of as stable rather than as partly open? Secondly, even if we can classify organizations according to the goals they attempt to realize, does this help us to examine the relationships between organizations and institutions? These two questions form the basis of the contribution of system theorists and structural-functionalist approaches[19] and some consideration must be given to them.

Talcott Parsons defines organization deductively by reference to the four functional problems of social systems.[20] The four system problems have already been referred to in Chapter 2, but can usefully be repeated. They are adaptation, goal attainment, integration, and pattern-maintenance or tension management. The first two are seen as arising when a unit[21] deals with its external problems, the second two its internal problems. Stress upon any one of these problems increases the strain on the others; the integration problem is increased by the requirement of adaptation. This is usefully illustrated in the Burns and Stalker analysis of pathological responses of mechanistic organization structure to changing technology and market instability. Equally the problem of pattern maintenance is increased by the requirement of goal attainment. The reverse stress upon internal functional problems increases strain upon the external ones. These four problems are used to show how systems and sub-systems are related. Parsons contends that each system develops sub-structures to cope with these problems and that these sub-structures themselves can in turn be analysed in terms of the four problems. Systems can be isolated functionally and sub-systems identified by their contribution to the functional problems of the system at the next higher level of

[19] See A. W. Gouldner, 'Organizational Analysis', in R. K. Merton *et al* (eds.) *Sociology Today*, Vol. II. New York: Harper, 1959.

[20] H. A. Landsberger in M. Black (ed.), *op. cit.*

[21] A unit can be an individual, role, group or system.

analysis. This approach was used in Chapter 2 where the economy was defined as the adaptive sub-system of society. It is from the isolation of the four problems at the level of society as a whole that organizations are classified comparatively.

Parsons considers that the organization as a social system is distinct from other types of social system by 'its primacy of orientation to the attainment of a specific goal.[22] The four system problems or goals relate to four broad types of organization. The four types are organizations oriented to economic production, to political goals, integrative organizations, and pattern-maintenance organizations. The first two types are self-explanatory but Parsons does interpret them in a wider sense than their usual definition. Thus whilst the firm is the obvious type concerned with the goal of economic production, this in the widest sense refers to 'adding value' and not only physical production. Organizations concerned with political goals not only include 'the organs of government' but less obviously orientation to political goals refers 'to the attainment of valued goals and to the generation and allocation of power in society'. Integrative organizations are concerned with the 'adjustments of conflicts and direction of motivation to the fulfilment of institutionalized expectations' and include legal institutions, political parties, interest groups and social control organizations such as hospitals. Pattern maintenance organizations are those primarily concerned with cultural, educational and expressive functions; in this category are included churches, schools and family—given that the last is highly differentiated.

Not only may organizations be differentiated according to the goals which they serve in relation to the total social system but also, Parsons suggests, according to five variables which in combination provide a basis for systematic differences between organizations. These five variables are technical and institutional levels of the organization, technology,[23] 'the fact that different organizations obtain and use different imputs differently', 'location in different functional sectors of society', and 'articulation between levels'.[24] These variables are distinctive in that they begin to ask the kinds of questions which the inductive approach has recognized as important to a formal theory of organizations. They represent a distinct shift of emphasis in Parsons'

[22] T. Parsons, *Structure and Process in Modern Societies*, *op. cit.*

[23] It is questionable whether Parsons explores the scope of the problem as it has been understood in work organization theory.

[24] This articulation concept reinforces the suggestion contained in Chapter I, namely that organization may be thought of as referring to the power structure of social systems.

approach and although to explain each requires more space than available here, it is suggested that these systematic differences refer to problems already empirically located by the inductive approach.

The attempt to define the comparative basis of organizations in system terms has not been limited to Parsons; Argyris, amongst the neo-human relations theorists, has suggested an inter-organization approach which has as its central problem how the organization and the individual articulate with each other.[25] Prior to examining his approach, two points need to be noted: the theory is explicitly related to a notion of 'mental health' and the two polar types of organization he suggests derive from whether or not the organization is regarded as inhibiting or facilitating this; secondly, although claiming that analysis is applicable to all organizations, most of Argyris' own study has been of work organizations.

Argyris suggests that formal organizations and the individual are basically organisms or organizations at different levels of analysis and share five essential properties: (1) they consist of 'a plurality of parts' which (2) 'maintain themselves through their inter-relatedness' and (3) 'achieve specific objectives'. Whilst maintaining themselves and realizing particular goals they (4) 'adapt to the external environment' and (5) thereby 'maintain the inter-related state of parts'. From these five essential properties are drawn several propositions. The parts of the organization cannot be defined *a priori*—they may be individuals, groups or departments. The idea of inter-relatedness makes the 'part' organic. All systems possess manifest or latent goals, and since they are embedded in their environment, organizations as systems are subject to environmental influence.

One problem arising from the fact that organizations are embedded in an environment is that of defining where the organization ends and the environment begins.[26] A second is that of the 'prediction of future changes from present conditions when there is no necessarily constant relationship between input and output'. Finally, Argyris suggests that organizations as systems possess three 'core activities', namely, achievement of objectives, internal maintenance and external adaptation. This is not so different from Parsons' four system problems, but here the similarity ends. Argyris uses the five system dimensions of organizations to polarize the 'axiologically good organization'. Since

[25] C. Argyris, *op. cit.*

[26] Typically this problem has been regarded as a critical one for the organization-role level of analysis; see particularly, R. L. Kahn *et al.*, *Organizational Stress*, New York: Wiley, 1964, pp. 99–123.

this presupposes his notion of mental health this latter requires further examination.

The individual is regarded as mentally healthy when 'he has access to all parts of his experience and his self', functions as a totality and is able to influence his adjustment and adaptation. Thus the 'psychologically healthy individual strives to be self-responsible, self-directed and self-motivated', aspiring towards problem solving and the decrease of compulsive behaviour. This notion of mental health is seen as referring to capacity not actuality; actuality is controlled by the organization. It is the 'axiologically good organization' which permits this psychic actualization.[27]

This good organization is defined in terms of five variables. Firstly, 'the whole is created and controlled through the inter-relationships of all parts'. In the organization this means that parts possess autonomy and reciprocity and that feedback exists so that 'each part has that degree of influence that it requires to maintain itself and perform its functions in the whole'. 'Awareness of a pattern of parts' rather than individuals occupying roles only being aware of a 'plurality of parts' is the second variable. The third is 'influence over internally oriented activities'. This is the notion of participant or horizontal-organic authority structures rather than authoritarian or vertical-mechanistic authority. The fourth variable, 'effective problem solving', refers to the internal functioning of the organization and Argyris suggests that this effectiveness increases as the organization recognizes its problems, locates the relevant alternatives, and for each alternative accurately estimates the consequences and chooses the most satisfactory alternatives. The fifth variable concerns the organization's relationship to its environment and is the extent to which 'core activities' are influenced by past and future considerations and not only by the present.

Argyris recognizes that organizations have different histories and that how these condition the variables defined is subject to empirical analysis. However he maintains that, in so far as the 'axiologically good organization' is consonant with individual mental health, it is so because the latter is positively related to 'the capacity of the individual to produce, to be committed, creative and flexible' and that these factors themselves will 'enhance the organization's capacity to achieve its goals, survive and grow'.

[27] The value assumption explicit in Argyris' analysis is based upon a notion of what work ought to mean and what the 'good man' in industrial society ought to be. Both are disputable.

SUMMARY: DIRECTIONS AND PROBLEMS

The group of five theorists and their approaches to the comparative analysis of work and non-work organizations raise a number of critical problems. Some have been identified by Mayntz[28] and more recently by contributors to March's handbook.[29] The object of this introductory chapter is not to resolve these, far less to explore some of the more sophisticated aspects of philosophical and psychological concern. But there are two problems of obvious general concern which can usefully be touched upon. The first is how far the inductive-factor approach and the system approach are mutually exclusive. The second problem is the contribution of role analysis.

The first can be dealt with quite briefly. The organization can be said to exist in so far as systems of social relationships are structured by variables existing independently of those who occupy positions in those systems. What these variables are requires an examination and substantiation by the formal-inductive approach adopted by Pugh and Hickson and what is required is an extension of this approach to the comparative analysis of work and non-work organizations. This presumes that the variables themselves are agreed upon and that they are comparative. The central sociological problem, however, is that they are not agreed upon. For example, organizations do have different goals but whether these can be deductively established at all levels by reference to the functionalist conception of the societal system problems is questionable. (This is recognized by Parsons in referring to '*primacy*' of orientation.) It could be contended with as much justification that differentiation according to political or power interest group formation and the decision-making processes of organizations is the central variable.[30]

The functionalist classification of organizations according to goals is disputable as providing comparative variables for organization analysis. Formal-inductive analysis in the Pugh and Hickson sense is also questionable because some non-work organizations (for example, the Psychiatric Unit) are not stable structures in their sense. In fact the strength of the system theorist position is just in the assertion that organizations defined functionally are dynamic and at least partly

[28] R. Mayntz, 'The Study of Organizations', *Current Sociology, A Trend Report*, Vol. 13, No. 3, 1966.

[29] J. G. March (ed.), *Handbook of Organizations*, Chicago: Rand McNally, 1965.

[30] If a conflict model of organizations was under consideration this would be a tenable starting point. See particularly for the problem of decision-making J. G. March and H. A. Simon, *Organizations*, New York: Wiley, 1958.

open. It is as easy to say that functionalist and formal approaches are right as to say that they are both inadequate, and that this inadequacy itself stems from the distinct attempts of each to meet the requirements of theory construction and empirical adequacy respectively. Given that the goals organizations attempt to realize can provide a basis for a comparative approach to organization differences, the question to be answered is how differences in goals relate to structural dimensions. As Etzioni has already suggested, the answer would appear to be that of 'power means' and possibly, as the other theorists have suggested, technology is a second key dimension. This can certainly be upheld in the case of work organizations.

In so far as organizations are systems of social relationships objectively structured as roles then one solution to the comparative problem is to ask what are the dimensions most significant for comparative role analysis. Many variables have been examined[31] but of these, two clusters seem particularly important; firstly the kind, degree and range of *autonomy in role performance;* secondly the kind, degree and range of *role content and role means*. These are not mutually exclusive or inter-dependent. The first refers to the familiar authority variable and concerns freedom to decide the 'what' as well as the 'how' of the role. The second concerns the type and stability of behaviour required in the organizational role.

Although the usefulness of these concepts cannot be fully expanded here, some indication can be given of their comparative possibilities. The assembly-line worker and the teacher not only do different things in their work roles but the specificity of what they do also varies. The teacher's work role is less specific than that of the assembly-line worker, and the manager's as specific as that of the teacher. The diffuseness or range of the content and means tends to be associated with how much autonomy the person in the role has to choose what he does, as well as how he does it. The tendency towards the completely non-autonomous role is found when what the person does, as well as how he does it, are prescribed by highly specific role content and stable authority structure. There is a tendency for autonomy-diffuseness and non-autonomy-specificity to be associated, but as objective dimensions they are not necessarily dependent. For example, the scientist in the work organization, concerned with applied research, may have a highly specific work role content but possess a large degree of autonomy in determining the how of what he does. This is a function of the expertise he brings to the role. The same parallel may

[31] B. J. Biddle and E. J. Thomas (eds.), *Role Theory: Concepts and Research*, New York: Wiley, 1966.

be applied to the social worker. Diffuseness of content may well accompany choice about what is done, as well as the means used.[32]

Although such differences may be traced to the organization structure, given the goal differences already noted as a basis for classifying types of organization then many of the problems of induction-deduction and occupational classification could be resolved by extending role analysis. If role analysis were extended and generally applied to supplement formal-inductive analysis then it would be easier to assess how far role systems are comparative. Role analysis in the subjective sense of how the person fits in with the particular demands of his organization role—a central problem for the comparative theorist—could also be related to the comparative role differences already noted.

It would be comforting to suggest that there is a comparative theory of organizations. There are only approaches, but these suggest that a fully integrated body of theory and research findings in this field is not as remote as some have suggested.

[32] For a further discussion of specificity and autonomy see D. J. Hickson. 'A Convergence in Organization Theory', *Administrative Science Quarterly*, Sept, 1966, pp. 224-237, and M. A. Smith, 'Process Technology and Powerlessness', *British Journal of Sociology*, Mar. 1968.

8

Industrial Management

FOLLOWING an outline of the historical background to management in Britain, this chapter presents a sociological approach to management structure and behaviour in work organizations with illustrations from major research findings.

Historical Background

During the course of this century, management has emerged as a distinct occupational grouping throughout industrialized nations. This emergence has been a function of increasing scale, capital intensification and technical complexity in industry, and has been associated with a diffusion of share-ownership in privately owned firms.[1] As mentioned in Chapter 2, a general trend in industry has been the increasing proportion of managerial, white-collar and technical staff to manual employees. Management, in fact, has tended to become differentiated from both ownership and other employees.

Differentiation from ownership has given rise to the concept of a 'divorce of ownership from control'. This concept has received wide publicity and has aroused considerable interest in the goals and motivations of the new industrial 'controllers'.[2] However, the significance of the trend has probably been exaggerated. The abdication of their responsibilities by an expanding shareholder public has been a voluntary process. By no means all large British firms, and very few

[1] R. Bendix, *Work and Authority in Industry,* New York: Wiley, 1956, Chapter 4; F. Harbison and C. A. Myers, *Management in the Industrial World,* New York: McGraw-Hill, 1959, Chapter 6.

[2] A review of the literature is contained in W. L. Baldwin, 'The Motives of Managers, Environmental Restraints, and the Theory of Managerial Enterprise', *Quarterly Journal of Economics,* May 1964, pp. 238–256.

small ones, have passed from extensive owner-control.[3] Moreover, there is no conclusive evidence that the extent of direct ownership control is a major determinant of the type of policies followed by a company, or that a managerially controlled firm can in the long run disregard the interests of shareholders and the capital market they represent. Finally, the unity of interests and actions between managers at a national level implied by theories of the 'managerial revolution' (and which may be evident on occasions of exterior political pressure) is by no means the general rule during the everyday course of business.

Management has also become increasingly differentiated from other employees. As a separate managerial social stratum has developed, so entry to its ranks has become increasingly selective, especially in terms of required educational qualifications. Thus the proportion of senior managers with a university education has risen considerably faster in both Britain and the United States over the last few decades than has the proportion of graduates in their populations as a whole.[4] Studies of British managers' backgrounds indicate that men with higher educational qualifications and social origins are today very heavily represented in managerial positions.[5]

Among managers themselves, awareness of possessing a distinct occupational identity was manifested in the establishment of special institutes, training courses, conferences and literature. Several institutes associated with management were established in Britain shortly before and after the First World War—the founding of the Institute of Industrial Administration in 1920 is an important example. Such institutes reflected a view that managers required their own quasi-professional associations apart from existing employers' organizations. The literature, conferences and training courses which developed from the same period were devoted both to the exposition of new management techniques and to the formulation of an ideology to support and guide the new occupational grouping.[6]

[3] P. Sargant Florence, *Ownership, Control and Success of Large Companies*, London: Sweet and Maxwell 1961.

[4] Acton Society Trust, *Management Succession*, London, 1956, p. 15; W. L. Warner and J. C. Abegglen, *Big Business Leaders in America*, New York: Harper, 1955, p. 47.

[5] D. G. Clarke, *The Industrial Manager—His Background and Career Pattern*, London: Business Publications, 1966, Chapters 3 and 4; R. V. Clements, *Managers—A Study of their Careers in Industry*, London: Allen and Unwin, 1958.

[6] E.g., J. S. Lewis, *The Commercial Organisation of Factories*, London: Spon, 1896; E. Cadbury, *Experiments in Industrial Organization*, London: Longmans, 1912; J. Lee, *Management*, London: Pitman, 1921; O. Sheldon, *The*

The ideology tended to present managers as professional, rational experts. Managerial professionalism would marry technical expertise with impartiality; in this way managers could be left free to represent and reconcile the interests of other parties to industry. Claims of this nature, which can be understood primarily in terms of legitimating the trend towards managerial control, were expressed most vigorously when management was first establishing its separate social identity and in periods when there were particularly severe threats of industrial intervention from the labour movement or from the state.

The more technical aspects of management literature covered a range of new and rather specific techniques—such as work study—as well as discussion on the broader issues of organization and motivation. In so far as this second area involved assumptions concerning values and interests, it provided the ground on which ideology and technique tended to meet in management thought. Management writings on behaviour and organization are frequently categorized for the sake of simplicity into two broad theories: (i) 'classical' theory and (ii) 'human relations' or neo-classical' theory. The former is chiefly associated with the work of F. W. Taylor, Henri Fayol and their students.[7] The human relations approach is normally linked with Elton Mayo and his successors, although its antecedents are to be found in the writings of Mary Parker Follett, British Quaker employers such as Edward Cadbury and Seebohm Rowntree, and several other pioneer management thinkers.[8] Human relations and those aspects of classical theory concerned with shop floor operations are discussed in the following chapter.

A SOCIOLOGICAL VIEW OF MANAGEMENT

The Nature of Management

Research during the last two decades has indicated that the stereotypes of management employed by early theorists were over-simplified. In fact, management as a concept cannot be satisfactorily defined in

Philosophy of Management, London: Pitman, 1923. Lectures given at an early conference are recorded in B. Muscio (ed.), *Lectures on Industrial Administration*, London: Pitman, 1920.

[7] F. W. Taylor, *Scientific Management* (collected works republished by Harper, 1947); H. Fayol (ed.) *General and Industrial Management*, London: Pitman, 1949, also more recent works by L. Urwick and E. F. L. Brech.

[8] For works of Mayo and his school see Chapter 9. Also M. P. Follett, *Dynamic Administration*, London: Pitman, 1941; J. Child, 'Quaker Employers and Industrial Relations', *Sociological Review*, Nov. 1964, pp. 293–315.

simple one-dimensional terms. Not only can management be analysed at different levels ranging from the total economy to particular organizations and departments, but it can also be viewed from different perspectives. Harbison and Myers have identified three such perspectives: (1) management as an economic resource performing a series of technical functions comprising the organizing and administering of other resources; (2) as a system of authority through which policy is translated into the execution of tasks; and (3) as an élite social grouping acting as an economic resource and maintaining the associated system of authority.[9]

Existing definitions of management tend to reflect its particular facets. For instance, Fayol gave an early definition in terms of what he considered to be management's five essential technical functions: 'To manage is to forecast and plan, to organize, to command, to co-ordinate, and to control.'[10] Barnard placed greater emphasis on management as a social process. His 'functions of the executive' were to maintain a system of organizational communication, to secure essential efforts from individuals, and to formulate a purpose for the organization.[11] Wilfred Brown's more recent definition draws attention to management as a system of formal authority. The manager in Brown's view is 'a member of an organization who has subordinate to him authorized roles into which he can appoint members and determine their work; he is accountable for his subordinates' work in those roles.'[12]

While it is analytically useful to distinguish the various aspects of management, it is also important to recognize their inter-dependence. In particular, management in an organization cannot be fully understood in terms of its formally defined functions without due consideration of the social system through and within which managers have to work. This social system may involve managers in several sets of relationships—with groups largely 'external' to an organization (such as customers, shareholders, trade union officers and government officials), with non-managerial employees and with other members of the managing group itself.

[9] F. Harbison and C. A. Myers, *op. cit.*, pp. 19–20. A useful short discussion on the various usages of the term 'management' is that by W. H. Wesson, 'Management' in J. Gould and W. L. Kolb (eds.) *A Dictionary of the Social Sciences* (UNESCO 1964), pp. 403–404.

[10] H. Fayol, *op. cit.*, pp. 5–6.

[11] C. I. Barnard, *The Functions of the Executive*, Cambridge, Mass.: Harvard University Press, 1938, p. 217.

[12] W. Brown, *Exploration in Management*, London: Heinemann, 1960, p. 50.

Managerial 'technical' performance can be affected by the nature of this organizational social system. Burns, for instance, has presented detailed evidence of the way in which what he calls political and status considerations in industrial concerns may reduce the effectiveness of their 'working organization'.[13] The nature of management in modern society is paradoxical in the sense that while consensus exists over the invaluable contribution of management as an economic resource, there is opposition to particular managerial actions in particular situations and even serious conflicts within management structures themselves. An explanation lies in the fact that industrial organizations are fundamentally co-operative associations but with a membership of different groups possessing divergent as well as shared goals and orientations—in this light they can be considered as plural societies. Thus a key managerial problem is the reconciliation of demands made upon an organization by various groups and individuals (including managers) who are in a position to obstruct the implementation of technically requisite changes.

In short, management is a many-sided concept. The perspective with which sociologists are primarily concerned is that of a continuous social process maintained (at organization level) by a managerial group within a structure of diverse industrial roles. We now review research on management structure and behaviour illustrating this perspective of management.

Management Structure

The management of all but extremely small industrial organizations is normally differentiated (i) structurally in the form of a 'vertical' status hierarchy and a 'horizontal' specialization of work roles and (ii) culturally in the form of the different occupational values, aspirations and social images held by managers. The extent and form of managerial differentiation will vary in different situations; it is, however, significant for the understanding of managerial behaviour patterns and will be seen to underlie many of the findings reported in this chapter.

Management structure in most industrial organizations can be categorized as follows:

(1) *senior management:* directors, and departmental heads in large firms.

(2) *middle management:* generally occupying positions betweeen (1) and (4) in the 'line' hierarchy (see below).

[13] T. Burns and G. M. Stalker, *The Management of Innovation*, London: Tavistock, 1961.

(3) *staff specialists, technicians, and other 'experts':* scientists, engineers, lawyers, personnel officers, etc.

(4) *first-line supervisors:* foremen, sometimes chargehands and section leaders.

Groups (1), (2) and (4) form the backbone of most management hierarchies and are frequently referred to as 'line' management—that is, they perform functions which have direct responsibility for achieving a company's prime objectives rather than functions existing chiefly to provide advice and service. (A firm may, however, have a director representing staff departments, while 'line' management will normally be horizontally as well as vertically sub-divided.) We saw in Chapter 5 how there are certain parallels between this line management hierarchy and the social stratification system in the wider community.

The existence of roles positioned on the 'boundaries' of management, whose incumbents may possess social ties with groups outside management, provides an instance where cultural factors may reinforce structural differentiation in management. Executive directors, industrial scientists and foremen occupy such boundary roles; they are often subject to conflicting loyalties and may suffer elements of 'role-strain' as a result. A full-time executive director may have to represent conflicting requirements of shareholders for high dividend pay-out and of the firm (as represented by its management) for high profit retention. Moreover, decisions reached on a majority basis by the Board of Directors may conflict with the interests of the firm as he sees them through the eyes of his own department.[14] Industrial scientists may face hostility from line managers with a markedly different training and outlook to their own, and experience personal strain from the conflict between their professional value of pursuing research for its own sake and the requirement of line management that their work be confined to projects promising some commercial return.

Foremen have aptly been described as 'men in the middle', caught between conflicting demands of higher management and operatives.[15] Their role-strain is heightened by the fact that in Britain most foremen are skilled workers who have been appointed to a position where they are now expected to represent managerial requirements. In practice, foremen have been found to represent their operatives' point of view against that of management, particularly where union organiza-

[14] Cf., W. Brown and E. Jaques, *Glacier Project Papers*, London: Heinemann, 1965, Chapter 9.

[15] W. F. Whyte and B. B. Gardner, 'The Man in the Middle: Facing the Foreman's Problems', *Applied Anthropology*, Spring 1945, pp. 1–28.

tion was weak.[16] Occupying a boundary role, foremen have also been labelled the 'marginal men' of industry.[17] This marginality has been increased in many large firms by the growth of technical specialisms such as work study, production control, personnel management, and by the tendency to by-pass foremen in industrial relations negotiations—all of which have contributed to an erosion of the foreman's managerial power and status.

The attempt to maintain unity between these various managerial groups generally results in the formalization of authority and work roles into an organization structure. 'Classical' management theorists were well aware of the problem posed by the conflicting principles of 'unity of command' and 'specialization by function'—of the need to integrate and yet to differentiate within management structure. The solution advanced by these early theorists amounted to a blueprint for organization structure based on a set of 'principles' assumed to be valid and effective for all situations. In so far as these principles stressed hierarchic dependence and role definition, they tended to produce what has been called a 'mechanistic' type of management system (see Chapter 7).

Recent research has indicated that the organizational blueprint advanced by classical theory is in many cases not appropriate to a firm's needs. Instead, suitable management structures and systems have to be chosen in the light of factors such as plant technology and the rates of change experienced by organizations. For instance, Woodward, on the basis of a study of 100 firms in South-east Essex, has suggested that the management structure most appropriate to a firm's requirements depends on its plant technology.[18] She classified the firms in her survey according to their overall technological complexity—(i) unit and small batch production, (ii) large batch and mass production, (iii) process production. She found that a number of structural characteristics showed a direct relationship with technical advance; for example, the length of the line of command and the ratio of managers to total personnel. With other structural features the greatest divergence lay between the extremes of technology (taken together) and mass production in the middle. Moreover, firms' manufacturing

[16] K. E. Thurley and A. C. Hamblin, *The Supervisor and his Job*, London: HMSO, 1963, pp. 15–16.

[17] D. E. Wray, 'Marginal Men of Industry: the Foremen', *American Journal of Sociology*, Jan. 1949, pp. 298–301.

[18] J. Woodward, *Industrial Organization: Theory and Practice*, London: Oxford University Press, 1965. Also *Industrial Organization: Behaviour and Control*, London: Oxford University Press, 1970.

cycles and the nature of relationships between their task functions—development, production, marketing—differed according to technology. The number and nature of management decisions that had to be made were also found to depend on technical demands. More decisions had to be made in unit production than in other technologies, all of them relatively short term and almost equal in importance. In mass production, decisions were more varied both in character and importance, while in process production decisions were fewer but committed firms further into the future. Woodward does not present all her findings with statistical rigour, but some have received support from an investigation of twenty-four companies by Blain.[19]

Investment in complex production technology may itself be conditional upon a number of economic considerations, among them the degree of stability in an organization's technical and market context. Regarding this context, Burns and Stalker's research has indicated that a 'mechanistic' management system with clearly defined roles and an emphasis on hierarchical authority might perform effectively in relatively stable technical and market conditions, but that a less formally structured 'organismic' system proved more successful in coping with changing and evolving conditions. Using American research data, Litwak suggested similarly that formal and hierarchy-based relationships would be more effective when dealing with routine, uniform tasks; and that informal relationships based on a more horizontal pattern of authority would be more effective with non-uniform tasks.[20] Morse and Reimer in a study of supervision over routine clerical tasks found that 'hierarchical' non-participative supervision backed by work study gave higher productivity, though lower employee morale, than did 'autonomous' participative styles.[21] Other research has shown that there is no necessary correlation between organizational effectiveness and individual principles advanced by classical management theory, such as a strictly limited 'span of control'.[22]

Apart from the discredit now attached to classical theory on purely practical grounds, social science research has led to the realization that organizations themselves are systems of continuing social interaction the subtlety and complexity of which could never be accounted

[19] I. Blain, *Structure in Management*, London: NIIP., 1964.

[20] E. Litwak, 'Models of Bureaucracy which Permit Conflict', *American Journal of Sociology*, Sept. 1961, esp. pp. 178–179.

[21] N. C. Morse and E. Reimer, 'The Experimental Change of a Major Organizational Variable', *Journal of Abnormal and Social Psychology*, Jan. 1956, pp. 120–129.

[22] I. Blain, *op. cit.*, p. 28; R. Stewart, *The Reality of Management*, London: Heinemann, 1963, pp. 31–35.

for in terms of a static framework of formal responsibilities. The following section brings together some of the research into managerial behaviour which is already coming to enrich our understanding of industrial organizations as dynamic, 'living' systems.

MANAGERIAL BEHAVIOUR

Managers' Use of Time

A collection of studies into patterns of managerial work, ranging from Swedish and German top managers to American first-line supervisors, agree that the largest proportion of managers' time is normally spent in some form of conversation. Burns, studying ninety-four managers in ten British firms, found that more time was spent talking the faster the rate of technical and other changes in a firm—an indication of the pressure towards an 'organic' management system under conditions of rapid change.[23]

The management stereotypes suggested by earlier theorists are brought into question by findings that the content of managerial work can be highly variable and even erratic. Moreover, it seems that (for British managers at least) the picture of the 'organization man' sacrificing leisure and family life for the firm is largely a myth. Burns found that the average total commitment to work in his sample, including homework, business lunches, reading, and travel for the firm, was only 43½ hours per week. In a sample of 66 'middle managers' in 10 varied companies, Horne and Lupton found the average working week to be 44 hours.[24]

There is some evidence that managers' use of time varies according to their position in the company hierarchy. Going down the management ladder, the proportion of time spent with superiors increases, while there tends to be a large increase in interaction with peers. Indeed, it is becoming apparent that classical management theory greatly underestimated the extent and importance of 'horizontal' communication between organizational equals. Horizontal interaction chiefly serves a co-ordinative function. Horne and Lupton found that most of their middle managers spent about threequarters of their time on activities holding their organizations together—organizing, regulating, controlling. Dubin concluded from his review of research on managerial behaviour that horizontal co-ordination, together with

[23] T. Burns, 'What Managers Do', *New Society*, 17th Dec. 1964.

[24] T. Burns, *op. cit.*, p. 8; J. H. Horne and T. Lupton 'The Work Activities of Middle Managers', *Journal of Management Studies*, Feb. 1965, pp. 28, 30.

the gathering of information from lower levels of the organization, takes up the greater part of managers' time.[25]

Decision-making

Several studies have reported that a low proportion of managerial time is occupied in taking decisions—on average about 15%. However, these observations have not accounted for the whole decision-making cycle: they are based on a misleading distinction between the actual taking of a decision and the prior collection and assessment of data together with the subsequent review of the decision.

Dubin has reviewed the few available studies of particular high level management decisions. Although these were long-term decisions, Dubin suggests that in general the time scale over which decisions are reached tends to be very much longer than a merely formalistic analysis leads one to expect. Moreover, Dubin emphasizes the significance of the political factor in business decision-making, whereby the diverse interests of individuals and organizational groups are accommodated in the final decision. This political process accounts for the time taken to arrive at most major managerial decisions. Sayles, discussing managerial decisions of a more everyday nature, has also stressed that they form part of a continuous political process.[26] Decisions at this level are marginal adjustments rather than the all or nothing decisions envisaged by classical management theory.

Martin, studying a large American manufacturing company, found differences between decision-making at different levels of management.[27] Decisions at higher levels tended to have a longer time-cycle from the preliminary stages of arriving at the decision through to the eventual assessment of its correctness. Decisions at higher levels were also considerably less clear cut, contained more elements of uncertainty, and the stages in their decision cycle were more discontinuous. The longer time scale of decisions at higher management levels is empirical support for Jaques' contention that 'time span of discretion' —the maximum length of time between the taking of a decision and its review either by the decision-taker's superior or by some indirect mechanism—tends to increase as one goes up a company hierarchy.

[25] R. Dubin, 'Business Behavior Behaviorally Viewed', in G. B. Strother (ed.), *Social Science Approaches to Business Behavior*, London: Tavistock, 1962, pp. 24–25.

[26] L. R. Sayles, *Managerial Behavior*, New York: McGraw-Hill, 1964, Chapter 12.

[27] N. Martin, 'Differential Decisions in the Management of an Industrial Plant', *Journal of Business*, Oct. 1956, pp. 249–260.

This concept, Jaques claims, provides a valuable measurement of responsibility and level of work.[28]

Conflict within Management

Patterns of conflict within management structures have been given considerably less attention than those between management and labour. While conflict within management may result from a clash of personal ambitions, sociologists have looked for the social and structural characteristics in industry which regularly induce conflict, and which may underlie what at first sight appears to be merely a personal quarrel. For example, Dalton concluded from a study of line/staff conflict in three American factories that it was largely attributable to the following largely structural features: (1) differences in function between the two groups; (2) differences in age, formal education, potential occupational ceilings, and social status group affiliations; (3) the need of staff groups to justify their existence; (4) fear by line managers that expanding staff groups would undermine their authority; and (5) the fact that aspirants to higher staff positions could gain promotion only through the approval of influential line managers.[29] Burns and Stalker suggest several factors underlying a lack of co-operation between industrial scientists and line managers—the threats posed by the former as change agents, inappropriate organizational arrangements, and the generally different orientations of the two groups. These orientations approximate to those Gouldner has conceptualized as 'cosmopolitan' and 'local'.[30] A cosmopolitan orientation entails little loyalty to a particular local organization and considerable commitment to professional contact outside the organization—a local orientation is the reverse.

Line management departments may themselves hold different immediate objectives and criteria of performance which can encourage conflict between them. For instance, there may be conflict between production and marketing departments over delivery dates promised to, and the type of orders accepted from, customers. The effectiveness of production and inspection tends to be measured in terms of different criteria—low cost per unit and quality—which may generate conflict between the two functions. It is likely that inter-departmental conflict of this kind will be most marked in large-batch production firms

[28] E. Jaques, *Equitable Payment*, London: Heinemann, 1961.

[29] M. Dalton, 'Conflicts between Staff and Line Managerial Officers', *American Sociological Review*, June 1950, pp. 342–351.

[30] A. W. Gouldner, 'Cosmopolitans and Locals', *Administrative Science Quarterly*, Dec. 1957–March 1958, pp. 281–306, 444–480.

having highly differentiated organizations and considerable pressures associated with the economical production of large quantities of often complex products.

There may also be marked antipathy between managers occupying different levels in the organizational status structure or possessing different career prospects. Clements found that antagonism towards higher management could unsettle lower managers so much that they considered taking jobs elsewhere. Burns found, in a factory which stressed promotion as the mark of success, that older managers lacking further promotion prospects formed themselves into cliques which acted as a protective counter-system against the prevailing norms and values of the organization.[31]

In sum, conflict within management may be regarded as a normal feature of organizational process, deriving from pressures imposed by the structuring of work situations and from the expectations held by persons in those situations. This conflict is not necessarily 'pathological'; it may contribute usefully to the adaptation of organizations in the face of changing circumstances, and may provide an insurance against managerial stagnation.

Managerial Mobility

The most recent study of British managerial mobility is by Clarke. While this is limited to industry in North West England, the author does compare his findings with earlier studies in order to suggest probable trends.[32]

Entry to management in highly industrialized societies is becoming more selective in terms of required educational qualifications. Clarke comments that, given the present social composition of pupils at different British educational institutions, 'the "average manager" is increasingly coming from a middle-class home and has received a grammar school and university education.' Over time, relatively fewer managers are being recruited either from the highest social backgrounds or from manual and routine white-collar ones, while relatively more are coming from families where the father is himself a manager or supervisor. There appears to be a trend away from managers starting their careers as apprentices, manual workers or

[31] T. Burns, 'The Reference of Conduct in Small Groups: Cliques and Cabals in Occupational Milieux', *Human Relations*, Nov. 1955, pp. 467–486.

[32] D. G. Clarke, *The Industrial Manager—His Background and Career Pattern*, London: Business Publications, 1966. Previous British studies are G. Copeman, *Leaders of British Industry*, London: Gee, 1955; Acton Society Trust, *Management Succession*, London, 1956; R. V. Clements, *op. cit.*, 1958.

clerks, and towards starting as technicians, draughtsmen, laboratory assistants or trainees.

The mobility of managers between firms appears to be quite low (a third of the managers in Clarke's survey had been employed in one firm), and those with higher educational qualifications tend to be the least mobile. Where managers had moved between firms, this was generally before the age of forty. However, there was considerable mobility within firms and this often involved geographical mobility. Almost half Clarke's sample had held their present position for under five years, while over a quarter had changed functional areas during their career—chiefly to production and (not quite so often) to sales. Many of the changes to production had been from technical work. Despite the changing patterns of recruitment, there appears to have been little change in managers' career patterns once inside the industry.

CONCLUSION

Management structure and behaviour are both integral parts of the dynamic functioning of organizations, a social process which Dalton has described as 'a shifting set of contained and ongoing counter phases of action'.[33]

Management as part of organizational process can be systematically analysed and understood. It can be understood in terms of the interaction between the structure of managerial work roles and the occupants of those roles. We have seen how management structure is likely to be influenced by contextual factors such as plant technology and the rates of change experienced by organizations. Managerial behaviour may be understood not only in the light of work roles, but also of factors such as managers' personal values and aspirations, pressures brought on them by the behaviour of their superiors, and their previous experience and statuses in an organization.

Research carried out within this perspective has indicated the deficiencies in the over-simplified prescriptions offered by a great deal of previous management theory. By the same token, social science analysis provides a means to mitigate or accommodate, on the basis of understanding, a number of important practical problems faced by managers—such as the less constructive forms of industrial conflict, resistance to technical and administrative change, and the design of effective systems of rewards and incentives.

It must be admitted that social science research in the field of

[33] M. Dalton, *Men Who Manage*, New York: Wiley, 1959, p. 4.

industrial management is still sparse, and that many managers remain to be convinced of the practical as well as theoretical importance of such research. In fact, there is a need not only to extend the researches mentioned in this chapter, but also to study emerging areas of great future consequences—for instance, the organizational impact of the new direct access information technology.

9

Human Relations and the Work Group

In this chapter we shall examine the origins and development of the Human Relations movement and attempt to assess its contribution to industrial sociology and particularly to the study of work groups. This contribution has been varied and significant, but is nevertheless typically characterized by certain important limitations and has frequently been criticized. Two recent studies of work groups provide examples of more satisfactory approaches.

Early Approaches to Human Behaviour at Work

A proper understanding of the contribution of the Human Relations movement, and of its strengths and weaknesses, demands that some attention be given to earlier approaches to human behaviour at work. These were the background against which the Human Relations studies developed from the late 1920's onwards. The three most important of such approaches were perhaps those of classical economics, scientific management and early industrial psychology and physiology.[1]

Put oversimply, the assumptions economists made about the behaviour of individuals, as entrepreneurs or workers, included the following: that individuals acted in isolation and without regard for others; that they acted in pursuit of their own interests so as to maximise their income; and that they acted rationally, logically relating means and ends. This view was made notorious when Elton Mayo, the 'father' of the Human Relations movement, attacked it as the 'Rabble Hypothesis': 'Natural society consists of a horde of unorganized individuals; every individual acts in a manner calculated to secure his own self-preservation and self-interest; every individual

[1] See G. Friedmann, *Industrial Society*, Glencoe: Free Press, 1955.

thinks logically and to the best of his ability, in the service of this aim.'[2]

These assumptions by economists were developed in the elaboration of macro-economic theories, and Mayo may have misunderstood their purpose.[3] However, this sort of approach to human motivation and behaviour was also accepted by many others including the proponents of Scientific Management, whose work it underlies. F. W. Taylor and his associates attempted to apply scientific methods to industrial work. Their approach included the assumptions that men could be related to their work rather as machines to be made as efficient as possible; that, properly used, incentives would evoke more, and more efficient, work by the employee; and that the financial rewards from the increases in efficiency which would result from the use of Scientific Management could be used to increase the income of both managers and workers and thus secure the harmonious co-operation of both groups.

Taylor's ideas aroused a great deal of controversy and opposition even at the time. One early source of criticism was the work in industry of physiologists and psychologists investigating such phenomena as fatigue and monotony. Taylor's assumptions about human behaviour were criticised in the light of findings regarding, for example, the effects of cumulative fatigue and the variations in abilities between workers. Such research stressed the importance of the 'human factor', and directed attention to environmental conditions —heating, lighting, colour, hours of work and rest pauses—and to their effects on workers' behaviour.

THE HAWTHORNE EXPERIMENTS

The Human Relations movement arose as a reaction against all these approaches with their individualistic and over-rational emphasis, and their tendencies to explain workers' behaviour as a response to their environment defined largely in material terms. The investigations at the Hawthorne Works of the Western Electric Company in Chicago between 1927 and 1932 have been widely reported.[4] They developed out of lighting experiments in the earlier tradition, the investigators

[2] Elton Mayo, *The Social Problems of an Industrial Civilization*, London: Routledge 1949, p. 37f.

[3] S. Krupp, *Pattern in Organizational Analysis*, New York: Holt, Rinehart, 1961; V. W. Bladen, 'Economics and Human Relations', *Canadian Journal of Economics and Political Science*, 1948, pp. 301–311.

[4] For the full account see: F. J. Roethlisberger and W. J. Dickson, *Management and the Worker*, Cambridge, Mass.: Harvard University Press, 1939. For an excellent summary: H. A. Landsberger, *Hawthorne Revisited*, Ithaca, N.Y.: Cornell University Press, 1958, pp. 4–27.

being forced to take social factors increasingly into account to explain their results. The three main stages were a study of a small group of women workers in the Relay Assembly Test Room, attempting unsuccessfully to relate output to hours of work and rest pauses; an extensive interviewing programme using increasingly non-directive methods; and observation of a group of men in the Bank Wiring Observation Room for a period of six months, revealing complex 'informal' organization and group control over levels of output and other forms of behaviour.

The historical importance of these studies is undoubted. They demonstrated the practicality and value of empirical research in industrial organizations. It could fairly be claimed as a result of the experiments that the earlier approaches were shown to be inadequate: 'many significant variations (in output) could not be related to physical working conditions alone'; 'the efficiency of a wage incentive was so dependent on its relation to other factors that it was impossible to consider it as a thing in itself having an independent effect on the individual'.[5] The worker could no longer be regarded as a socially isolated individual who acted rationally and independently of his fellows to maximise his income. The existence of 'informal' organization had been 'discovered', and group influences on workers' behaviour and output had been observed in great detail, though the varying nature of such influences was less clearly accounted for. In addition, the study outlined the beginnings of a model of the factory as a social system, and of the worker as 'social man'.

The Hawthorne Experiments have probably been more often discussed than any other single piece of research in industrial sociology. In a comprehensive review of this literature Landsberger has shown that much of it can best be regarded as criticism of the use which has been made of the research results, the ways in which they have been popularized, and the general approach and philosophy of the Human Relations 'school', rather than as criticism of the Experiments themselves. It is true that some of the methods used appear unsophisticated in comparison with subsequent developments in this field, and in particular studies of single, especially selected small groups were relied upon as the basis for far-reaching generalizations. It has also been shown that many of the observations and results are capable of alternative interpretations to those given by the investigators.[6] Nevertheless the

[5] Roethlisberger and Dickson, *op. cit.*, pp. 160–1.

[6] For example: T. Lupton, 'Social Factors Influencing Industrial Output', *Man*, 1956, 49, pp. 55–59; M. Argyle, 'The Relay Assembly Test Room in Retrospect', *Occupational Psychology*, 1953, pp. 98–103.

studies performed the important functions of showing that certain basic assumptions were inadequate and of directing subsequent research to a number of hitherto neglected factors.

We shall therefore consider first the directions taken by subsequent research in this tradition, and the general philosophical position taken up by Mayo in particular, before considering the criticisms which can be made of this approach to the analysis of industrial organizations.

RESEARCH ON HUMAN RELATIONS IN INDUSTRY

The empirical enquiries pursued by those who are in the Human Relations tradition can be roughly grouped into three main streams. Each of these has a starting point in problems raised by the Hawthorne Experiments, but each includes perspectives gained from other sources.

Firstly, both the Relay Assembly Test Room and the Bank Wiring Observation Room demonstrated the importance of group influences on individual behaviour at work, though the analysis of why the former group co-operated so well with management and the latter obstructed management's goals was less satisfactory. In particular the Test Room results directed attention to the ways in which supervisors behaved and to communications between management and workers. Such lines of thought were strengthened by the work of Lewin and others experimenting with 'authoritarian', 'laissez faire' and 'democratic' styles of leadership in small groups, in which the most satisfied groups were those with democratic leadership.[7] The relationship of these variables —styles of leadership, productivity, morale and group participation in decision making—were tested in a number of experimental and quasi-experimental studies.

Well known and typical examples of such studies include the experiment in a clothing factory in which Coch and French found that groups allowed to participate in planning changes of work showed less resistance to the changes, higher levels of output achieved more quickly after the change, and less dissatisfaction than groups which had not been allowed to participate in this way.[8] In studies of railway permanent way gangs and of groups of office workers in an insurance company, members of the Michigan Survey Research Center found that groups with high output had employee-centred supervisors who

[7] See, for example: R. White and R. Lippitt, 'Leader Behaviour and Member Reaction in Three "Social Climates" ' in D. Cartwright and A. Zander (eds.), *Group Dynamics*, London: Tavistock, 1953, pp. 585–611.

[8] L. Coch and J. R. P. French, Jr., 'Overcoming Resistance to Change', *Human Relations*, 1948, pp. 512–532.

saw their role as involving leadership functions and spending time on specifically supervisory tasks, and, in the case of the clerical workers only, exercised general rather than close supervision. Such high-producing groups tended to have greater pride in their own work groups, but, at least in the case of the railway workers, were less satisfied with the job itself than the low-producing groups.[9]

These and many other studies appeared to reinforce some of the possible interpretations of the Hawthorne Experiments, but further research has been less conclusive. For example, some workers allowed to participate in making decisions have tried to expand the scope for them and have come up against management's refusal to delegate more authority.[10] In another study the response to supervisory practices varied markedly with the influence the supervisor had with his superiors.[11] The inadequacy of a narrowly based social-psychological framework for enquiry has been increasingly apparent, and more recently both critics and proponents of this type of research have stressed the need to consider explicitly the broader organizational and social setting.[12]

The second group of studies has been concerned with continuing the analysis of the structure and functioning of small groups in industry, extending this to the whole organization, and developing an analytical framework for this purpose around the study of 'interaction'. For example, Homans, using the basic concepts of 'action', 'interaction' and 'sentiments', has reanalysed the Bank Wiring Observation Room data, and by comparing it with other small group studies has tried to develop general propositions about small groups.[13] Whyte, in a large number of studies in industry and using a fairly similar approach, has explored problems which have been neglected by many Human Relations researchers. These include union-

[9] D. Katz *et al.*, *Productivity, Supervision and Morale among Railroad Workers*, Ann Arbor, Mich: Survey Research Center, 1951; D. Katz *et al.*, *Productivity, Supervision and Morale in an Office Situation, Part 1*, Ann Arbor, Mich.: Survey Research Center, 1951; or see: R. L. Kahn and D. Katz, 'Leadership Practices in Relation to Productivity and Morale' in Cartwright and Zander, *op. cit.*, pp. 612–628.

[10] H. L. Wilensky, 'Human Relations in the Workplace', in C. M. Arensberg *et al.*, *Research in Industrial Human Relations*, New York: Harper 1957, pp. 25–50; M. Bucklow, 'A New Role for the Work Group', *Administrative Science Quarterly*, 1966, pp. 59–78.

[11] D. C. Pelz, 'Influence: a Key to Effective Leadership in the First-line Supervisor', *Personnel*, November 1952.

[12] See, for example, Wilensky, *op. cit.*; E. H. Schein, *Organizational Psychology*, Englewood Cliffs, N. J.: Prentice Hall, 1965.

[13] G. C. Homans, *The Human Group*, London: Routledge, 1951.

management relations and the different patterns of interaction which developed as the pattern of industrial relations changed towards 'industrial peace'; the effect of type of work flow and of changes in technology on interaction and sentiments within groups and organizations; and the consequences of the use of incentive payment systems on individual, group and plant-wide bases.[14] Other leading 'interactionists' have claimed that this approach provides a dynamic analysis which makes it possible to predict and to come to grips with the movement of a social system.[15]

Thirdly, Lloyd Warner and his associates have extended Human Relations research in another direction. In the course of a major study of a New England community, referred to as Yankee City, they analysed the place of the industrial organization in the local community and the ways in which it may be affected by wider economic and social changes. Thus their explanation of a strike was in terms of both 'internal' and 'external' factors: there had been changes in the occupational structure and skill hierarchy within the factory, the development of mass markets and absentee ownership, and a change in the status of factory management in the local community.[16]

THE INFLUENCE OF ELTON MAYO

The Hawthorne Experiments were first popularized by Elton Mayo and his interpretation of their significance and that of a small number of other studies of working groups has had a very wide influence.[17] Mayo was alarmed by the social disorganization and conflict which he saw as deriving from the breakdown of the 'established' society of pre-industrial period. Man's scientific and technical discoveries had led to the break-up of this established society but his knowledge of social processes was inadequate for the creation of an 'adaptive' society. Mayo saw the solution to the problem of *anomie* in the modern world in the development of social skills, particularly by managers and administrators, and the maintenance by them of the 'spontaneous

[14] W. F. Whyte, *Pattern for Industrial Peace*, New York: Harper, 1951, *Money and Motivation*, New York: Harper, 1955; *Men at Work*, Homewood; Ill.: Dorsey Press, 1961.

[15] C. M. Arensburg and G. Tootell, 'Plant Sociology: Real Discoveries and New Problems', in M. Komarovsky (ed.), *Common Frontiers of the Social Sciences*, Glencoe: Free Press, 1957, pp. 310–337.

[16] W. L. Warner and J. O. Low, *The Social System of the Modern Factory*, New Haven: Yale University Press, 1947.

[17] E. Mayo, *The Human Problems of an Industrial Civilization*, New York: Macmillan, 1933; and *op. cit.*

co-operation' in industry which the Hawthorne Experiments and other research had shown was possible. Within industrial organizations in cohesive small work groups, men could find the sense of belonging and the social purpose which they had lost. He saw conflict as pathological; it could and must be resolved by developing a sense of shared purpose within industrial organizations and the realization that social satisfactions as well as material rewards were of importance to the worker. He also saw 'an eager human desire for co-operative society' as persisting in the ordinary person and thought that willing co-operation could be secured by skilful leadership.

These ideas have not only provided an underlying philosophy for much research in industry, but they have also influenced managerial practice, and perhaps even more, managerial ideologies, as Bendix and others have pointed out.[18] In Britain and the United States especially much Human Relations training has been undertaken, particularly of supervisors, though experimental and other studies have generally failed to demonstrate that such training achieves the desired results.[19] The limitations of training based on Human Relations ideas, and the ambiguity of many of the results of research designed to test Human Relations propositions, have added to the growing body of criticism of this tradition of investigation.

THE LIMITATIONS OF THE HUMAN RELATIONS TRADITION

Human Relations, narrowly conceived as merely the Hawthorne Experiments or the work of Mayo, or so all embracing that it includes almost everybody who ever mentions 'human relations in industry', has been subjected to recurrent barrages of criticism over the last twenty-five years. As will be obvious from the references made so far, not all points of criticism are equally applicable, or indeed applicable at all, to all the investigations within this tradition. With this reservation in mind, however, we may try to summarize the criticisms which have been made and to see why more recent studies of work groups have taken a rather different direction.

The most obvious target for criticism has been Mayo's sweeping analysis of the problems of industrial societies. This has been attacked

[18] R. Bendix, *Work and Authority in Industry*, New York: Wiley, 1956; L. Baritz, *The Servants of Power*, New York: Wiley, 1960.

[19] J. H. Goldthorpe, 'La conception des conflits du travail dans l'enseignement des relations humaines', *Sociologie du Travail*, 1961, pp. 1–17; E. F. Harris and E. Fleishman, 'Human Relations and the Stability of Leadership Patterns', *Journal of Applied Psychology*, 1955, pp. 20–25.

as involving a misinterpretation of the past, of the nature of pre-industrial society, and more important as seeing only one of the many possible solutions to the problems of the present.[20] Many of the factory workers studied by Mayo and his colleagues were first or second generation immigrants living in rapidly growing and changing urban areas, and their 'anomie' cannot be seen as a necessarily permanent feature of industrial societies. Even if this analysis were correct, Mayo ignores the possibilities of building social integration and belongingness through associations such as churches, communities and trade unions rather than the factory and the work group within it. In his writings research on small groups is applied to the analysis of whole societies without any apparent awareness of the different problems and levels of explanations involved.

However, most writing in the Human Relations tradition is not concerned with such problems, even though some support may be given to Mayo's general approach. Nevertheless, much of it suffers from limitations which are connected with the weaknesses of the Mayo perspective. The most central of these limitations is in the analysis of the causes and nature of industrial conflict. Human Relations researchers, from the Hawthorne Experiments onwards, have successfully shown how interpersonal and intergroup conflicts within industry can arise from ineffective communications and 'bad' supervisory or management practices. They have appeared less aware of the limitations of such an analysis and of the existence of conflicts of interest between groups which derive from their positions in the structure of industrial organizations and industrial societies.[21] The emphasis on the social satisfactions to be gained from membership of a cohesive work group has distracted attention from the question of economic rewards, from the conflict of interests over the distribution of the income of the enterprise as wages or profits and the power differential between management and workers. Mayo's concern for harmony in the wider society has been paralleled by a concern with co-operation and equilibrium within the factory, and a failure, on the whole, to see the functions of conflict, its inescapability in a 'free' society, and to see 'that it is precisely the *freedom* to conflict which establishes the

[20] See, for example, H. L. Sheppard, 'Approaches to Conflict in American Industrial Sociology', *British Journal of Sociology*, 1954, pp. 324–341; C. Kerr and L. Fisher, 'Plant Sociology: the Elite and the Aborigines', in M. Komarovsky (ed.), *op. cit.*

[21] H. L. Sheppard, *op. cit.*, and 'The Treatment of Unionism in "Managerial Sociology"', *American Sociological Review*, 1949, pp. 310–13; R. C. Sorenson, 'The Concept of Conflict in Industrial Sociology', *Social Forces*, 1951, pp. 263-7. The Bank Wiring Room study is only a partial exception to this point.

boundaries within which the actual conflicts can be contained'.[22] Analysis has centred on the integrating rather than the differentiating factors within the plant, and as such has been one-sided.[23]

Many of the other criticisms which can be made are related to this fundamental one. Thus, with some exceptions (such as Whyte's and Warner's work referred to above) trade unions and industrial relations have been largely ignored in Human Relations research. Unions did not exist in the Hawthorne Works in 1927—though it has been claimed that at that time and later the Company spent considerable sums to prevent their organization;[24] but subsequent research cannot always make that claim. Unions have been difficult to accommodate within the Human Relations approach, except perhaps as associations oriented to management goals, and there has been no clear examination or understanding of their 'origin, functions or essential nature'. Similarly, analysis of industrial relations has tended to remain within the plant, or even be limited to face-to-face relations. It is difficult to explain within a Human Relations frame of reference why certain industries should have consistently high and others consistently low strike records;[25] a monopoly of Human Relations skills by those in certain industries seems improbable, but broader social and economic factors have rarely been considered.

A further and often justified criticism of Human Relations research is that it 'stops at the plant gates'. The relationship of internal and external influences on an individual's behaviour at work is discussed in considerable detail in *Management and the Worker*, and Warner's study was explicitly concerned with industry-community relations. However, much research, mostly notably that in the social-psychological tradition, has considered work groups and worker-supervisor relations in isolation from the wider organizational and social setting. Even where the organizational setting has been seen to be important, there has rarely been recognition of the economic and social forces outside the plant which constrain the behaviour of management and workers within it. The influence of the depression on the Hawthorne Experiments was noted but neither at the time, nor later, were its implications for the understanding of organizational behaviour fully

[22] R. Bendix and L. Fisher, 'The Perspectives of Elton Mayo', in A. Etzioni (ed.), *Complex Organizations*, New York: Holt, Rinehart, 1961, pp. 113–26.

[23] G. Friedmann, 'Philosophy Underlying the Hawthorne Investigations', *Social Forces*, 1949, pp. 204–9, and *op. cit.* pp. 315–25.

[24] Landsberger, *op. cit.*, pp. 51–2.

[25] C. Kerr and A. J. Siegel, 'The Inter-Industry Propensity to Strike', in A. Kornhauser *et al.* (eds.), *Industrial Conflict*, New York: McGraw-Hill, 1954 pp. 188–212.

worked out. Human Relations research has tended to be unsatisfactory in just the areas which require explicit and systematic consideration of factors outside the organization.

These limitations of the Human Relations approach have been ascribed to failure by the investigators to recognize and make explicit their own value orientations, their preferences for collaboration and stability in society rather than conflict and change.[26] Furthermore, this bias is linked to an acceptance of management's definition of the goals of the enterprise; the divergent and conflicting values of groups in industrial societies have not been recognized.[27] This is related to both the choice of problems for research (neglect of unions and industrial relations, for example) and the implications of research for managerial practice. Defenders of Human Relations research can argue justifiably that there has been an important contribution to social scientific knowledge and understanding, but it is undeniable that intentionally or not much of the research, because of the value orientations of the researchers, has served to increase management's control over workers. The most notorious example of this is perhaps the personnel counselling programme at Hawthorne Works, which was introduced in the light of the success—as a means of releasing tension—of the non-directive interviewing during the Experiments. The Wilenskys claim that 'counselling has helped protect management's freedom to promote, downgrade, transfer, train, discipline, lay off, apply a variety of rewards and sanctions (with a minimum of interference from a relatively co-operative union)—in short it has helped the company retain its control over the worker'.[28]

Secondly, the limitations of the Human Relations analysis of industrial enterprises can be related to basic theoretical and methodological weaknesses. Much of the research has been empirical, with few theoretical developments and limited use of the theories and concepts of others. In particular, levels of analysis and explanation have not been clearly distinguished. Human Relations studies have been particularly concerned with inter-personal relations in small groups. The enterprise has been conceptualized, and in a limited way analysed, as a social system, but on the whole the organizational and

[26] Bendix and Fisher, *op. cit.*; W. A. Koivisto, 'Value, Theory and Fact in Industrial Sociology', *American Journal of Sociology*, 1953, pp. 564–72; Kerr and Fisher, *op. cit.*

[27] W. E. Moore, 'Current Issues in Industrial Sociology', *American Sociological Review*, 1947, pp. 651–7; Koivisto, *op. cit.*

[28] J. L. and H. L. Wilensky, 'Personnel Counselling: The Hawthorne Case', *American Journal of Sociology*, 1951, pp. 265–80.

institutional levels of analysis have been neglected. Yet an adequate explanation of behaviour in work groups demands an awareness of the influence of organizational and institutional factors; otherwise particular findings will be generalized without regard to context. Conversely it is not possible to assume that, for example, face-to-face relations between workers and an individual manager or supervisor are necessarily paralleled by, or influenced by the same factors as, worker-management relations, or, even more so, union-management relations at the level of the organization or of the total society. Yet all this often seems to be implicit in the Human Relations approach.

RECENT STUDIES OF WORK GROUPS

Two recent investigations can provide examples of the ways in which some of the limitations of the conventional Human Relations approach have been largely overcome, at least as far as studies of work groups are concerned. Significantly both of them have an important comparative element.

Firstly, Sayles has attempted to differentiate and categorize work groups primarily in terms of their behaviour—the methods they evolve to solve their day to day problems, their response to management and supervision, and the type of people they recognize as their leaders.[29] On the basis of interviews and observational and other data relating to 300 work groups in thirty plants in a variety of industries in the United States, four types were distinguished. In each case the behaviour described remained characteristic of the group over a period of time even when personnel changed.

'Apathetic' groups (e.g. many unskilled workers) had low levels of grievance activity, no clear leadership and little internal unity; they were not ranked as very co-operative or as high producers by management, and played little part in union affairs. The rather more united 'erratic' groups (e.g. automobile assembly line workers) were easily aroused into grievance activity but of a poorly controlled sort with behaviour which was inconsistent in terms of their own apparent goals; leadership was often highly centralized, and such groups, ranked as unsatisfactory employees by management, played an active part in the union especially in the organizational stages. With the highest level of grievance activity, 'strategic' groups (e.g. key groups such as welders) continuously, consistently and rationally used pressure in

[29] L. R. Sayles, *Behaviour of Industrial Work Groups*, New York: Wiley, 1958, p. 5f.

support of their interests; with a very high degree of internal unity, they participated strongly in union activities, supplying much of the leadership, but, in the long run, also had relatively good records as employees with management. The most stable groups were the 'conservative' ones (e.g. garment cutters and toolroom personnel); highly united internally and ranked as the most satisfactory employees by management, they used restrained pressure to redress specific grievances and were generally less active in union affairs.

The explanation of these differences was sought not in the social and leadership skills of supervision and management, but in the ways in which social relations were affected by the technology and division of labour within a plant. These factors strongly influenced both the relations between groups and their internal structure. The level of grievance activity appeared to be related primarily to the status of the work group in relation to other groups in a plant—those in the middle ranges were the most active; and the type of pressure exerted appeared to be related to the internal organization of the group—activities were well planned and controlled in groups with independent operations.

Sayles's analysis, which also included accounts of changes of behaviour over time, will no doubt be modified in the light of further research. Nevertheless it represents an important step forward in the investigation of work group behaviour. Differences in behaviour were examined systematically and related to the social structure and system of production of a plant, so that behaviour is seen in its organizational context. There was no assumption of harmony of interest between management and workers; indeed the analysis focused on manifestations of conflict and encompassed union activity. Work groups with common economic interests and a desire to change the situation to secure their interests were distinguished from the 'informal' groups, to which Human Relations researches drew attention as a source of social satisfaction and stability for the worker.

A second example comes from a study of two workshops by means of participant observation, as a result of which its author, Lupton, was forced to consider not only the organizational context but also factors external to the factories concerned in order to explain the behaviour of work groups.[30] In both workshops workers were paid on an incentive scheme, but whereas in one case (a workshop assembling small transformers) the workers did not respond as intended by management but

[30] T. Lupton, *On the Shop Floor*, Oxford: Pergamon, 1963.

used an elaborate 'fiddle' to stabilize their earnings and effort, in the other (a waterproof garment factory) no such regulation of output occurred. The difference was not due to any superiority of one incentive scheme over the other from the workers' point of view, or to any differences in social satisfactions or in leadership skills or efficiency on the part of management and supervision.

The explanation lay, Lupton argued, partly in the differences which were 'internal' to the work group. For example, in the garment workshop where the workers, contrary to Lupton's expectations, did not attempt to exercise a measure of collective control over the operation of the incentive scheme, the productive system was characterized by a minute breakdown of operations and a short time span. The method of wage payment was straight piecework with no complex system of allowances providing opportunity for a 'fiddle'. Friendship cliques and sociable groupings did not coincide with production groupings and no collective attitude to output and earnings developed, the predominant attitude being 'looking after number one'. However, these factors, all of which were not found in the other workshop studied, and what Lupton referred to as a lack of a 'will to control' on the part of the workers, were related to external factors, the social and economic environment of the workshop. The industry consisted of small firms in an unstable and highly competitive market; seasonal unemployment was common; labour costs were a relatively high proportion of total costs; the trade union was weak, especially at the workshop level. There was no opportunity for an 'indulgency pattern' such as existed in the other workshop with its completely different social and economic environment.

Given the differences of environment and of social relations and production systems within the workshops, the behaviour of the respective groups of workers appeared to Lupton to represent a realistic appraisal of their interests in the light of the knowledge available to them. In contrast to the analysis of the Bank Wiring Observation Room data, there was no implication that the behaviour was only to be explained in terms of a 'logic of sentiments'.

Thus these two recent studies provide illustrations of more adequate investigation and analysis of work group behaviour. Identity of interests of management and workers was not assumed, and explanation was extended to environmental factors outside the group, and in Lupton's case outside the organization altogether. His approach has stimulated systematic and comparative investigation of such 'contextual' factors and their interrelations which should provide a valuable basis for future studies.[31] Finally, both writers give an important place in their explanations to the relationship of technology and social relations, which we consider in more detail in the next chapter.

[31] D. S. Pugh *et al.*, 'A Conceptual Scheme for Organizational Analysis', *Administrative Science Quarterly*, 1963, pp. 289–315; see Chapter 7 for a discussion of this.

10

Technology, Technical Change and Automation

THE relationship between technology and social structure in industry, between the productive process and the social relations which surround it, has been an important theme in the sociological analysis of industrial societies. This focus of interest is particularly emphasised in the parallel concern with the social consequences of technical innovations. In this chapter we shall examine some of the attempts which have been made to categorize types of production system and to relate aspects of the social structure of the enterprise to these types. We shall then consider the impact of changes in technology, and in particular of those changes which are commonly called 'automation', and the reactions of those subject to such changes. Though much work remains to be done, certain general trends can be described with some confidence.

One of the diffculties in this field is that terms are very often used in vaguely defined ways. 'Technology' is sometimes used to refer narrowly to the particular machines and equipment employed in production, but can more usefully be held to refer also to the body of knowledge and ideas which makes possible the employment of such machines and equipment. It is important to bear in mind too that technology is itself a social product and not something separate with an autonomous development.

TECHNOLOGY AND SOCIAL STRUCTURE IN INDUSTRY

Living as they did during periods of rapid industrialization and technical change, many of the 'classical' sociologists were concerned with the problem of the relationship of technology and social structure. Thus, for example, in Marx's analysis of the development of human society a vital part was played by 'the change and development of the material means of production, of the forces of production'. 'The mode of production of material life conditions the social, political and intellectual life process in general'.[1] As another example, Durkheim's study of *The Division of Labour in Society* includes a highly perceptive account of the social consequences of the use of certain types of production system in what he terms 'abnormal forms' of the division of labour.[2] More recently writers such as Friedmann have explored the consequences of developments in industry, in part caused by technological changes, which lead among other things to extreme specialization and fragmentation of tasks.[3]

Though such approaches provided illuminating overall views of developments in modern industrial societies, they were too general to encompass adequately the great variety of situations which more detailed research revealed. One of the most welcome trends in recent years has been the various attempts which have been made to distinguish different types of production system and to identify the social characteristics which appear to be associated with each of them. Such attempts have been confined mostly to manufacturing industry, but it is encouraging to note that independent analyses have produced remarkably similar conclusions.

We have already referred in Chapter 8 to Woodward's distinction between unit and small batch production, large batch and mass production, and process production, and her scheme, which in its fullest form comprises nine stages and two mixed types, is based on differences in technical complexity and the degree to which it is possible to exercise control over manufacturing operations and to reduce areas of uncertainty.[4] Woodward points out that these types form stages in the chronological development of industry towards increasing standardization of products and increasing mechanization. This view is also shared by Touraine and Blauner whose work is discussed below. However, it is not to be taken to mean that the development is in any sense inevitable or unilinear, or that a firm using process production methods is necessarily 'progressive' or a firm making varied products in small quantities is in any sense 'back-

[1] K. Marx and F. Engels, *Selected Works*, Vol. I, Moscow: Foreign Languages Publishing House, 1958, pp 90, 363.

[2] E. Durkheim, *The Division of Labour in Society*, Glencoe: Free Press, 1933, esp. Book 3.

[3] G. Friedmann, *The Anatomy of Work*, London: Heinemann, 1961.

[4] J. Woodward, *Industrial Organization*, London: Oxford University Press, 1965; and *Management and Technology*, Problems of Progress in Industry, No. 3, London: HMSO, 1958.

ward'. The appropriate production system depends on the objectives of the enterprise.

A French sociologist, Touraine, also distinguishes three main stages in the development of technology and sees them as arising from the interaction of two contrasting processes. On the one hand there is a disintegration of the worker's skill; the work previously performed by one man is broken down into its component parts. On the other hand such a process makes possible the mechanization of these tasks and the development of an integrated production process which is in a sense automatic. Thus one moves from the old system of work based on craft skills using universal or flexible machines to produce a diversity of products, through a transitional stage characterized by unskilled workers feeding machines or performing very few simple operations to produce standardized products, to automation where the worker superintends, records and controls rather than does direct productive work.[5]

The third writer, Blauner, outlines four types of technology which arise from the long-run trend to increasing mechanization and increasing standardization of the product. 'Craft' industries, such as printing, he argues, have no standardized product, and therefore no possibility for extreme rationalization and standardization, but are dependent on the skills of the craftsman. 'Machine minding' industries, such as textiles, show a considerable degree of standardization and mechanization with the worker feeding and supervising the machine. 'Assembly line' industries, such as the automobile industry, are based on extreme fragmentation of work and rationalization of production of standardized products. It is here that the problem of 'alienation' is most acute. 'Process' industries, such as chemicals, are the most highly mechanized, producing a uniform product in a continuous process.[6]

Before outlining the conclusions to be derived from these studies, certain reservations must be made which are emphasized by one or more of the authors themselves. Thus, though most industrial enterprises can be typified as having one or another type of technology, not all tasks in the organization will be similar to those typical of that type of production process (e.g. maintenance work in all types of industry involves craft skills) and some organizations may be difficult to categorize. None of the writers suggests that social relations are technologically determined; rather technology sets limits within which,

[5] A. Touraine, 'An Historical Theory in the Evolution of Industrial Skills', in C. R. Walker (ed.), *Modern Technology and Civilization*, New York: McGraw-Hill, 1962, pp. 426–37.

[6] R. Blauner, *Alienation and Freedom*, Chicago: University Press, 1964.

for example, management policies operate, and there is scope for different allocations of the tasks to be done. The scope for choice may itself vary with technology—Woodward, for example, suggests that it is greatest in large batch production situations. The economic structure of the industry may also lead to important differences, as may the character and expectations of the labour force.

The relationship which Woodward postulated between technology and management organization has been outlined in Chapter 8, and her conclusions are certainly supported by such evidence as is given on this aspect by Blauner's and Touraine's investigations. The latter two studies, however, consider in more detail other aspects of social relations in industry which are strongly influenced by technology, and in particular, the nature of the worker's task, its meaningfulness and the degree of his autonomy in carrying it out, social relations between workers, and management-worker relations.

In general it is suggested that the two extremes of the technological scale are in many respects more similar to each other than to large batch and mass production systems. Thus, the meaninglessness of the worker's tasks and his powerlessness are seen as greatest on the assembly line. In the 'craft' industry the worker has considerably autonomy, which may, as in printing, be reinforced by strong trade union organization, and he can see the relevance of his contribution to the final product. In process production the operative needs to understand the nature of a substantial part of the production system to carry out his task, which involves considerable responsibility. At the same time he may be able to vary the sequence of operations, and except in crisis situations he does not work under great pressure, output being determined by the capacity of the plant rather than the worker's effort.

Influences on social relations on the shop floor are complex and varied, (see Chapter 9). However, Sayles' research illustrates that knowledge of the place of work groups in the production system may be very important for the understanding of differences in their behaviour.[7] At a more general level the same conclusion regarding similarities between the two ends of the technological scale appears broadly true. In 'craft' industries workers may not be functionally interdependent but may share common craft identity and membership of an occupational community with some or all of their fellow employees. Because of a certain freedom of movement on the job they also have opportunity for the growth of social relations with other workers. At the other end of the scale process technology commonly

[7] L. R. Sayles, *Behaviour of Industrial Work Groups*, New York: Wiley, 1958.

demands teamwork from small internally structured work groups which can be a source of social satisfaction and make for a highly cohesive organization. 'Machine minding' and 'assembly line' technologies, in contrast, tend to tie the worker physically to the machine or place on the line and yet also leave him without membership of a clearly defined work group.

Management-worker relations are also, of course, influenced by many factors other than technology, but nevertheless it has been suggested that in this respect too the large batch/mass production systems, because of the nature of the situational demands of the production processes, give rise to more intense conflict than the two ends of the scale. It is in these situations that the pressures on the worker to maximise output tend to be greatest; with less standardized products, less complex technology, and more highly skilled workers it may be accepted that workers are unlikely to work well 'with a gun at their backs', and with process production there is generally less pressure and the plant itself can contribute 'a framework of discipline and control' which may be less resented than authority exercised by a superior.[8]

There are already a number of studies which provide support for the sort of analysis outlined so far. For example, Blauner was able to collate and compare fairly detailed reports on four industries representing his four technological stages. Perhaps the most intensively studied industrial situation has been the automobile assembly line, and the results achieved here can illustrate the strengths and weaknesses of this whole approach. These studies have emphasized that the worker's task, which is very much determined by the technology, is extremely limited and provides few if any intrinsic satisfactions. Its characteristics are a mechanically controlled work pace, extreme repetitiveness, a minimum of skill, predetermination of tools and techniques, a minute subdivision of the product, and the requirement of only surface mental attention. The worker has no control over his task and although he can see its relevance to the finished product, has little sense of a personal contribution. There are few obvious work groups and little interdependence. Social relations are hindered by pressure of work, noise and the physical layout. Nor can the foreman do very much to improve this situation by 'good' human relations practices. The chief attraction of such jobs is the relatively high pay. The division between management and workers tends to be accentuated, wage and skill distributions of manual workers are compressed

[8] E.g. Woodward, *Management and Technology, op. cit.*, p. 29.

with only marginal advancement possible, and opportunities for promotion from the shop floor are infrequent and uncertain.[9] Management-worker relations are bureaucratic, being defined in terms of formal agreements, and strikes and other manifestations of conflict tend to occur frequently.

This picture of the industry, which has been described as 'the classic symbol of the subjection of man to the machine',[10] has however to be modified in some important respects. Thus Guest has described how in the same plant over a period of three years performance, labour relations and interpersonal relations all improved markedly following the succession of a new manager and with no change in technology.[11] Studies of strikes in the motor car industry in Britain have shown considerable differences between different firms—presumably using similar technologies—and within the same firm over the post-war period, which suggests that other factors are of considerable importance.[12] Writers such as Friedmann and Chinoy have suggested that even on the assembly line job enlargement and job rotation may be possible and lead to an increase in intrinsic job satisfaction with no loss of output,[13] and Walker and his colleagues have argued that foremen can to some extent form their workers into a team and thus increase social satisfactions.[14] Finally Goldthorpe has described how the behaviour and attitudes of car assembly workers in one British plant were very different from those described in most other studies and has argued that such differences can only be explained in terms of the workers' orientation to work and their definition of their jobs and work situations which were derived from non-work aspects of their social lives.[15] The implications of these studies are not that technology is irrelevant in understanding social relations on the assembly line, but that it is not necessarily decisive.

[9] E. Chinoy, *Automobile Workers and the American Dream*, Garden City, N.Y.: Doubleday, 1955.

[10] C. R. Walker and R. H. Guest, *The Man on the Assembly Line*, Cambridge, Mass.: Harvard University Press, 1952, p. 9.

[11] R. H. Guest, *Organizational Change*, Homewood, Ill.: Dorsey Press, 1962.

[12] J. Bescoby and H. A. Turner, 'An Analysis of Post-war Labour Disputes in British Car Manufacturing Firms', *The Manchester School*, 1961.

[13] Friedmann, *op. cit.*, esp. p. 40–54; E. Chinoy, 'Manning the Machine—the Assembly Line Worker', in P. L. Berger (ed.), *The Human Shape of Work*, New York: Macmillan, 1964, pp. 51–81.

[14] C. R. Walker *et al.*, *The Foreman on the Assembly Line*, Cambridge, Mass.: Harvard University Press, 1956.

[15] J. H. Goldthorpe, 'Attitudes and Behaviour of Car Assembly Workers', *British Journal of Sociology*, Sept. 1966.

SOCIO-TECHNICAL SYSTEMS AND ORGANIZATIONAL CHOICE

Exploration of the interconnections of technology and social relations has also been considerably advanced by the work of the Tavistock Institute of Human Relations. Members of the Institute have developed the concept of a 'socio-technical system'[16] as a framework for their analyses:

'The concept of socio-technical system arose from the consideration that any production system requires both a technological organization—equipment and process layout—and a work organization relating to each other those who carry out the necessary tasks. The technological demands place limits on the type of work organization possible, but a work organization has social and psychological properties of its own that are independent of technology... A socio-technical system must also satisfy the financial conditions of the industry of which it is a part... It has in fact social, technological and economic dimensions, all of which are interdependent but all of which have independent values of their own.'[17]

A socio-technical system is regarded as an 'open' rather than a 'closed' system: it is related to its environment by exchange processes and is able to achieve a 'steady state' from differing initial conditions and in different ways.

The socio-technical system concept has been used in studies of coal mining in Britain and the cotton industry in India.[18] In both cases the technological situations were given and the results of the research were to challenge other assumptions which had guided the particular form of work organization adopted. These assumptions were that a high degree of task specialization was desirable; that workers could be treated as individuals in isolation; and that planning, coordination and control should be specialized functions divorced from the work group.

The mining study contrasted 'conventional' organization of the partially mechanized longwall system with 'composite' organization. The

[16] F. E. Emery and E. L. Trist, 'Socio-Technical Systems', in C. R. Walker (ed.), *op. cit.*, pp. 418–25.

[17] E. L. Trist *et al.*, *Organizational Choice*, London: Tavistock, 1963, p. 6.

[18] E. L. Trist *et al.*, *op. cit.*; E. L. Trist and K. W. Bamforth, 'Some Social and Psychological Consequences of the Longwall Method of Coal Getting', *Human Relations*, 1951, pp. 3–38; A. K. Rice, *The Enterprise and Its Environment*, London: Tavistock, 1963. For further discussion see R. K. Brown, 'Research and Consultancy in Industrial Enterprises', *Sociology*, 1967, pp. 30–60.

former involved the segregation of task groups from each other and the distribution of some forty men between seven distinct and highly specialized work roles, and three shifts, with five methods of payment. This system destroyed the quality of 'responsible autonomy' and the 'social balance' which had previously characterized the miner's role, and made for conflict within and between groups rather than the sense of interdependence which was needed for smooth functioning. Control and coordination had to be provided, with difficulty, by management and the wages system, and productivity and morale both tended to be low.[19]

In contrast 'composite' organization, with the same technology and similar underground conditions, led to greater work satisfaction, lower costs and increased productivity. The team of miners allocated men to shifts and tasks, and each miner experienced different roles and utilized several skills. Payment, with a bonus based on production, was on a group basis, and there was continuity of working so that men carried on with the next activity in the sequence when their own was complete. Despite its size the group could be self-regulating so that management no longer had to provide all coordination and control.

The analysis of weaving processes followed similar lines, but Rice was a consultant as well as investigator and able to introduce the changes himself and observe the improvements in quality and output.

The Tavistock Institute's studies accepted the central importance of technology for the sociological analysis of industrial situations. Their particular and valuable contribution has been to develop a theoretical model and to show in some detail how alternative forms of work organization within the same technological limits can lead to very different consequences. In this way they complement the description of general trends outlined in the previous sections.

TECHNICAL CHANGE AND RESISTANCE TO CHANGE

It will be clear from the discussion so far that major technical changes are bound to have important repercussions on social relations within industrial organizations, and indeed outside them as well. Where changes involve a transition from one type of production system to another Woodward suggests, on the basis of a number of case studies, that either changes take place to make social relations compatible with

[19] This analysis has received general support from other investigations, for example, W. H. Scott *et al.*, *Coal and Conflict*, Liverpool: University Press, 1963; J. H. Goldthorpe, 'Technical Organization as a Factor in Supervisor-Worker Conflict', *British Journal of Sociology*, 1959, pp. 213–30.

the demands of the new system, or predictable organizational problems arise due to resistance to change.[20] With some exceptions, detailed investigations of technical change have tended to be case studies and it is often difficult to assess their importance and value as a basis for generalization. Some valuable attempts have been made to systematize the work that has been done in this area,[21] but it is only possible to summarize here some of the factors which appear to be important and to give examples from a case study.

As Burns and Stalker have pointed out, industrial organizations can be conceived as comprising not only a 'working organization', but a 'status structure' and a 'political system' as well.[22] Technical changes are likely to affect not only the tasks to be done and work role relationships, but also the absolute and relative rewards and status of different groups and individuals, and their power and autonomy within the organization. In general it can be argued that resistance to change will occur when group or individual interests are threatened, including power and status in the organization. The degree to which this is true, and the particular manifestations of resistance to change will, however, be influenced by a variety of other factors.

The most important of these appears to be the definition of the situation by those affected, for example, the extent to which management's power to make changes is accepted as legitimate and/or likely to be used in employees' interests. Orientations to change tend to be more favourable among workers who are younger, more highly educated and with a higher occupational status.[23] The way in which changes are introduced is also important; conditions of secrecy, with no information until a late stage, are likely to give rise to greater anxiety and resistance to change than are cases where information is given, or even more so where those involved participate in planning the changes.[24] A major change in production system may well meet with more resistance than mere improvements of existing processes.

Since the days of the Luddites there has been opposition to changes

[20] Woodward, *Industrial Organization*, *op. cit.*, esp. pp. 209–40.

[21] A. Touraine *et al.*, *Workers' Attitudes to Technical Change*, Paris: OECD, 1965.

[22] T. Burns and G. M. Stalker, *The Management of Innovation*, London: Tavistock, 1961.

[23] A. Touraine *et al.*, *op. cit.*, esp. pp. 135–48; Department of Social Science, University of Liverpool, *Men, Steel and Technical Change*, Problems of Progress in Industry No. 1, London: HMSO, 1957, pp. 20–7.

[24] Cf., for example, E. Mumford, *Living with a Computer*, London: Institute of Personnel Management, 1964; L. Coch and J. R. P. French, 'Overcoming Resistance to Change', *Human Relations*, 1948, pp. 512–32.

which threaten the very existence of an occupational group, especially one with craft skills. With more advanced and integrated production systems it has been suggested that worker and union action tends to move to the level of the industry, or the whole economy, to safeguard their interests, rather than trying vainly to prevent changes in a particular plant.[25] It has also been suggested that change is more difficult to introduce in certain types of organization than others, in particular where the firm is either dominated by one group or thoroughly integrated and harmonious.

One of the best documented accounts of technical changes is a study of a North Wales steelworks.[26] Three distinct changes were introduced in a period of less than twenty years: a continuous strip mill in the place of hand rolling mills (from batch production to nearly full process production); new melting shops (an improvement of an existing process); and blast furnaces and coke ovens (a completely new process for this firm). All the changes proceeded very smoothly. They were introduced with full consultation with the unions. On the whole however no occupational group was seriously adversely affected by the changes. Redundancy was avoided because of the Second World War and, later, the expansion of the plant. Management prerogatives were clearly defined and accepted as legitimate, as was the seniority principle in promoting workers. Management-union relations were harmonious and workers' interests were effectively represented.

The changes had some important consequences for the social structure of the plant, which was still thought of as a family firm. Management organization became more complex and more specialized. More managers with technical qualifications were needed many of whom had to be recruited from outside, and this adversely affected the long run chances of promotion from the shop floor. Management organization was becoming more formal and systematic to deal with problems of coordination and control. The maintenance craftsmen became a more numerous and more important occupational group, and were dissatisfied because they felt their increased importance for the functioning of the plant was not recognized in terms of pay and status. The new strip mill involved major changes in tasks and in social relations for the operatives concerned, and it and the melting

[25] A. Touraine *et al.*, *op. cit.*, pp. 40–2, 87.

[26] Department of Social Science, *op. cit.*; W. H. Scott *et al.*, *Technical Change and Industrial Relations*, Liverpool: University Press, 1956; O. Banks, *The Attitudes of Steelworkers to Technical Change*, Liverpool: University Press, 1960. See also R. K. Brown, 'Participation, Conflict and Change in Industry', *Sociological Review*, 1965, pp. 273–95.

shop made less demands on skills based on experience and more on formal technical knowledge.

The status and pay of some workers was adversely affected *relative* to those previously comparable, and this was cause for complaint even where all had benefited in absolute terms. Home life was affected by the continuous shift working demanded by the technology, and this too was disliked. However, in general attitudes towards the changes were overwhelmingly favourable—most so among the staff, least so among maintenance workers. The study demonstrates that resistance to change or acceptance of it are not arbitrary or irrational, but can be explained with knowledge of the interests of those affected as they see them and of the other factors in the situation.

AUTOMATION

Popular interest in technical change in recent years has largely centred on automation. This term has been used to mean many things, and varied and contradictory assertions have been made as to the likely consequences of these latest technological developments. In fact automation is used to refer to three 'independent streams of technical progress': the use of transfer-devices to link machine tools in automatic production lines; the development of techniques of automatic control over manufacturing processes; and the use of computers for data processing, with the possibility of the extension of automatic control over complex operations.[27] The consequences for social relations within industrial organizations will depend on both the pre-existing situation and the type of automation introduced.

In general automation describes the same sort of technology and associated social relations as have been described above as process production. Thus mechanization and rationalization of processes are fully developed and operations centre on monitoring and maintaining the plant rather than direct production work. Work groups are small, responsible and relatively autonomous. Management-worker relations tend to be harmonious; the plant itself provides discipline and control and labour costs are a smaller proportion of total costs. Supervisory ratios tend to increase, management organization may become more complex and there is concern with the coordination of different aspects of production operations. At the same time rational decision making

[27] Department of Scientific and Industrial Research, *Automation*, London: HMSO, 1956, p. 1.

on the basis of knowledge and technical expertise becomes increasingly possible.[28]

There are some important exceptions to this general picture. As one example, the use of semi-automatic production systems, such as transfer machines in the car industry, has been shown by Faunce to result in the dispersal of work groups, greater pace of work, less frequent interaction with fellow workers, more pressure from supervisors and considerable strain involved in monitoring expensive equipment in a highly integrated process, even though the work was physically lighter.[29] In another case the introduction of a semi-automatic tube mill similarly meant that fewer workers were more widely dispersed, though the public address system was used for gossip as well as its intended purpose. Work roles were, however, highly interdependent because of the integrated process and strong group feeling developed. Initially the demands of operating the new plant caused considerable strain and anxiety, but this disappeared as the men mastered their new work environment. The initial period was also characterized by conflict regarding the incentive scheme, and though this was resolved, relationships with maintenance staff, who were not included but whose contribution was vital, remained troublesome.[30]

There are further exceptions when office automation—electronic data processing—is considered, though as yet there is only a limited amount of research available.[31] Some routine jobs disappear, but routine operations connected with the computer, for example preparing information for it, increase in number, and workers engaged on these, generally women, tend to be fairly sharply divided from those, generally men, in more responsible positions and with prospects of promotion. The introduction of computers may cause major modifications to the distribution of power in the firm, especially where they are used to perform qualitatively new tasks rather than just conventional tasks previously done by a large number of clerks, and their full

[28] See, for example, Blauner, *op. cit.*; F. C. Mann and L. R. Hoffman, *Automation and the Worker*, New York: Holt Dryden, 1960; *Three Case Studies in Automation*, London: Political and Economic Planning, 1957; F. E. Emery and J. Marek, 'Some Socio-technical Aspects of Automation', *Human Relations*, 1962, pp. 17–25.

[29] W. A. Faunce, 'Automation in the Automobile Industry', *American Sociological Review*, 1958, pp. 410–7.

[30] C. R. Walker, *Toward the Automatic Factory*, New Haven: Yale University Press, 1957.

[31] E. Mumford, *op. cit.*; E. Mumford, 'Clerks and Computers', *Journal of Management Studies*, 1965; W. H. Scott, *Office Automation*, Paris: OECD, 1965.

use may be resisted for this reason. Areas of uncertainty are reduced, more centralized decision making becomes possible, and there is greater dependence on experts associated with computer installation; the middle levels of management in particular may well lose control over a number of areas previously under their discretion.

This second, 'integrated', stage of office automation, combined with the technical advances associated with the other two streams of automation, may, it is suggested, lead to a type of industrial organization where authority is objectively and rationally used and decisions are not even in part the result of political bargaining within the enterprise. Though trends towards such a situation are observable, Willener, for example, has argued that at least two issues will remain: 'the suspicion that the system favours certain occupational or social categories'; and 'the problem of policy—the orientation given to the common activities'.[32]

Automation is best regarded as the latest of a long line of technical changes; study of it can add to our knowledge of the relationship between technology and social structure and of the processes of change in industrial organizations. This is not to deny, however, that the development of these various trends may lead to qualitatively new types of situation within industrial organizations.

[32] A. Touraine *et al.*, *op. cit.*, pp. 86–7.

11

Industrial Interest Groups

It is intended in this chapter to deal with part of the area of study called 'industrial relations' to complete a review of the sociology of industry on the organization-role level. Industrial relations, however, is an extensive field to which many others than sociologists have made contributions from different perspectives—economists, lawyers, psychologists, political scientists, and so on. There is considerable common ground between what these people study and what the sociologist studies, but the approaches are different. The student of industrial relations has a more limited field than the sociologist, but he can regard himself as inter-disciplinary within that field (i.e. he is part economist, part sociologist, part political scientist, and so on). The industrial sociologist has a wider field—which includes industrial relations—but he is not inter-disciplinary and concentrates on using the concepts and theory of sociology. He is particularly interested in *social relations within the enterprise* and the individual, group or collective *expressions of industrial interests.*

TRADE UNIONS AND PROFESSIONAL ASSOCIATIONS

Types of Interest Group

In the context of industrial relations, interest groups are a special kind of secondary group to be found in work organizations with authority structures. In addition to a structure and a form of organization, these groups have a programme or set of goals and a membership which includes among its activities the prosecution of group conflict. On the side of the employees there are trade unions and professional associations and on the side of employers there are those employers' associations which have industrial relations functions. Although the latter are sometimes regarded as 'the bosses' unions', the parallel is only partial, since the 'employer' is mostly already an organization, deriving strength from collective resources. Associations of employees, usually non-manual and sometimes called staff associations, which do not bargain with employers are not included here among interest groups.

There are good reasons for analysing the structure, functions and problems facing trade unions and professional associations separately, although they also have some common features. Trade unions are composed mainly of manual workers[1] and their chief function is to bargain with employers on behalf of members, a function which is only one of those performed by professional associations on behalf of *their* members. The main problems facing trade unions are the struggle for recognition by employers, the attempts to exert political influence on economic policies at national or regional level insofar as these affect the interests of members,[2] and various internal problems of organization and the need for more funds to extend activities.

Professional associations are composed of those whose employment has gained the recognized status of a profession, whether of the old-established type such as the law, medicine and the church, or of the newer type, including those highly-trained and qualified personnel without the traditional professional-client relationship (sometimes called 'quasi-professionals'). The functions of professional associations are varied: they bestow qualifications as an indication of competence or a licence to practice, they act as study associations, they regulate the professional conduct of their members, and they attempt to protect the interests and raise the status of their members. The main problems facing professional associations are preserving the relationship between the profession and the community, social control of members, adjusting to changes in the traditional professional-client relationship, and resolving (or at least containing) conflict between sections within the professional association.[3]

In the light of these differences it has been said that the functions

[1] But the total number of members in 'white-collar' unions in 1961 was estimated at over 2 millions, or more than 20% of all unionists (G. Routh, 'White-Collar Unions in the United Kingdom', in A. Sturmthal (ed.), *White-Collar Trade Unions*, Urbana: University of Illinois Press, 1966, p. 172); see also G. S. Bain, 'The Growth of White-Collar Unionism in Great Britain', *British Journal of Industrial Relations*, Nov. 1966.

[2] The influence of the trade union movement as a whole on government economic policies is exercised by the General Council of the Trades Union Congress, by trade union delegations to the Labour Party Annual Conference, and by individual trade unionist M.P.s.

[3] H. L. Smith, 'Contingencies of Professional Differentiation', *American Journal of Sociology*, Jan. 1958.

of professional associations and trade unions are mostly kept distinct, with neither showing signs of encroaching on the other.[4] This is true to the extent that many functions of professional associations are not shared by trade unions, but a tendency to convergence may also be seen. According to the Ministry of Labour, trade unions are 'all organizations of employees—including those of salaried and professional workers, as well as those of manual wage-earners—which are known to include among their functions that of negotiating with employers with the object of regulating conditions of employment.'[5] The fact that even this careful definition gives rise to a number of borderline cases between trade unions and professional associations adds weight to the view of Gross that, rather than seeking to define what is a profession and what is not, it is better to posit a profession-job continuum along which occupations are located according to the degree to which they exhibit various attributes.[6]

Trade Union Structure and Participation

Considerably more attention has been paid to the organization and membership of trade unions than to that of professional associations. A number of studies (chiefly American) have sought to make a sociological analysis of various aspects of trade unionism. Some of the main problems which have received attention are classification of types of union, the relation between external social and economic factors and changes in the structure of trade unions, and the maintenance of democracy in the functioning of unions.

The traditional classification of trade unions is based on a combination of type of skill and basis of organization into three groups of craft, industrial and general unions. *Craft* unions are the oldest type and are composed of workers performing the same or very similar industrial operation. *Industrial* unions cater for all, skilled and unskilled, within an industry, although the skilled workers tend to dominate this kind of union because they are more organized. *General* unions cater for workers in many industries and are often the result of amalgamations and federations of smaller unions. These types are

[4] K. Prandy, 'Professional Organization in Great Britain', *Industrial Relations* Oct. 1965.

[5] *Ministry of Labour Gazette*, Nov. 1952, p. 375. This definition may be compared with that of the Webbs before the role of trade unionism had widened to its present scope: 'a continuous association of wage-earners for the purpose of maintaining or improving the conditions of their working lives' (S. and B. Webb, *History of Trade Unionism*, London: Longmans, 1920, p. 1).

[6] E. Gross, *Work and Society*, New York: Crowell, 1958, p. 77f.

not always clear-cut; thus the Amalgamated Engineering Union is an industrial union for engineering, but a craft union for engineers in whatever industry they are employed. Also, this classification does not include the non-manual and technicians' unions.

Recognizing that the traditional threefold classification does not suffice to distinguish the main types of British trade unions, Clegg and his associates have suggested five groupings.[7] *General* unions are defined roughly according to the traditional classification. In preference to the old 'industrial union' which suggests one that includes all the workers in a given industry and no one else, *single-industry* unions describe those that are confined to, or have their predominant interest in, a single industry. A rigid application of the criterion of apprenticeship would unduly narrow the definition of 'craft unions', and so the term *skilled* unions is preferred by Clegg and includes those workers who acquire skill by promotion from grade to grade on the job. Craft unions which have changed the basis of their membership to include semi-skilled and unskilled workers constitute a fourth category of *ex-craft* unions. Finally, *white-collar* unions cater for clerical, supervisory, administrative and technical workers.

Another type of problem studied is that of how changes in industry or technology affect internal variables of unions such as size and composition of membership, relations between levels of organization and degree of bureaucracy. A theoretical model of trade union change has been put forward by Marcus which is used to order much existing research material concerning American unions and may well be usable with British unions.[8] Some conditions (increasing size and external pressures for hierarchical control) are seen to lead towards bureaucracy and oligarchy, while other pressures (independent sub-groups and legitimation of opposition[9]) contribute greater democracy. The structure of trade unions is affected by the degree of concentration of industry, its technology and the social status of its workers.

The question of democracy in trade union organization and prac-

[7] H. A. Clegg *et al.*, *Trade Union Officers*, Oxford: Blackwell, 1961, p. 14f; for a consideration of the differences between 'open' (expansionist) and 'closed' (restrictionist) unions, see H. A. Turner, *Trade Union Growth, Structure and Policy*, London: Allen and Unwin, 1962, p. 241f.

[8] P. M. Marcus, 'Organizational Change: The Case of American Trade Unions', in G. K. Zollschan and W. Hirsch (eds.), *Explorations in Social Change*, London: Routledge, 1964.

[9] Notably the unique two-party system in the International Typographical Union (S. M. Lipset *et al.*, *Union Democracy*, Glencoe: Free Press, 1956); see also J. R. Coleman, 'The Compulsive Pressures of Democracy in Unionism', *American Journal of Sociology*, May 1956.

tices has received considerable attention and is bound up with the problem of apathy of many members towards the running of their union's affairs. The degree of apathy varies among unions and low voting figures in elections for national officers and committees are often cited as evidence. Roberts gives detailed figures showing that the proportion voting is affected by industry, method and place of ballot,[10] and another study showed that in the National Union of Vehicle Builders 46% of members in branches of less than 100 voted, compared with 8% in branches of over 1,000.[11]

Another aspect of democracy in trade union organization concerns the vexed question of the 'closed shop'.[12] Broadly speaking, a closed shop means that a person cannot work in a particular job without being a union member. There are two types of closed shop: if a worker has to join the union before he can be engaged by the employer it is 'pre-entry'; if the employer is free to engage a non-unionist so long as he agrees to join the union it is 'post-entry'. Sometimes there is an arrangement by which labour must be engaged through the union, as in the newsprint industry. About one worker in six is in a closed shop, and among trade unionists in manual occupations it is one in two.

The question of participation in trade unions may be broken down into a study of the types of participant and of the *correlates* of participation. Tagliacozzo and Seidman[13] have distinguished seven types of rank-and-file union member according to their motivation to join the union and along a continuum ranging from the ideological to the unwilling: (1) the ideological unionist, in addition to being a devoted and enthusiastic member, sees union activities as having a broader goal of a different social order (2) the 'good' union man is also devoted, but has no desire to change the existing order (3) the loyal but critical member is still devoted but more critical of apathy and the leadership (4) the crisis activist only takes part in union activities when strikes or other crises arise (5) the dually-oriented member is more sympathetic to management and may hope to gain a supervisory position (6) the card-carrier or indifferent member joins only because

[10] B. C. Roberts, *Trade Union Government and Administration*, London: Bell, 1956, p. 226f.

[11] Political and Economic Planning, *British Trade Unionism*, London, 1955, p. 39.

[12] For a full account of this issue see W. E. J. McCarthy, *The Closed Shop in Britain*, Oxford: Blackwell, 1964.

[13] D. L. Tagliacozzo and J. L. Seidman, 'A Typology of Rank-and-file Union Members', *American Journal of Sociology*, May 1956.

his workmates have joined, and (7) the unwilling unionist joins because he has to in order to get or keep his job. The use of this typology could throw light on situations which are inadequately analysed by treating unionists as a homogeneous group.

Workplace Strategies

One of the most significant developments in trade unionism in recent years has been the growth of workplace bargaining and the increasing power of the shop steward movement. There are a number of reasons for this growth, but perhaps the key one concerns the role of informal organization in the industrial structure, as outlined in Chapter 9. In addition to whatever formal activities and practices occur, there are in most workplaces patterns of inter-personal relations over and above what is required by the formal structure. One aspect of this is the formal 'procedure' between management and unions for dealing with workers' grievances and claims, which is increasingly supplemented by the informal activities of shop stewards.[14]

Shop stewards are trade union representatives at the place of work. Some union rule books make no mention of stewards, and even those that do are not always an accurate reflection of the workplace situation. It has been suggested that the power of stewards has increased because their functions and responsibilities have never been clearly defined. This undoubtedly facilitates the activities of stewards but does not adequately explain why their increasing role in the industrial relations system has been largely accepted by other actors in the system. For the key to this we must look to the circumstances and motives of these other actors. As compared with taking a dispute 'through the procedure' there are advantages to both management and labour in settling it at workplace level. One result of involving higher levels is to increase the size of the staffs needed to process the grievances. From the union point of view, higher-level settlement increases the stability and binding power of the agreement and leaves less room for manoeuvre at local level.

The role of the shop steward has many features of sociological interest. He interacts with three sets of participants in the industrial relations system—his members (i.e. his fellow-workers), the full-time officers of his union, and members of management in the firm for which he works. His 'opposite number' on the management side is the foreman or first-line supervisor and most of his management

[14] W. E. J. McCarthy, and S. R. Parker, *Workshop Relations in Britain*, (Research Papers 10 for the Royal Commission on Trade Unions and Employers' Associations), London: HMSO, 1968.

contacts are on this level. The role he plays is thus divided into three sectors, and his skill as a negotiator and mediator is tested by his ability to satisfy the different demands of the groups he deals with. To his members he is someone who speaks up for them to management and wins better pay or conditions for them; to his union he is someone who carries out union policy at the workplace; and to management he is (according to the attitude of particular management members) someone who is a troublemaker to be mastered or a responsible mediator between themselves and the ordinary workers.

The 'ideal type' of a steward would combine each of these role sectors into an integrated whole. He would manage to reconcile the conflicting role expectations which each of the three groups has of him. In practice, however, most stewards consider their obligations to be *primarily* towards only one of these groups. Thus Miller and Form have characterized three types of steward as job- or management-oriented, union-oriented and employee-oriented.[15]

INDUSTRIAL RELATIONS

The Industrial Relations System

The term 'industrial relations' is used in two ways: in the all-inclusive sense it refers to all the relationships between managers and employees within industry and in the community; in a more restricted sense it refers only to collective relations between unions and employers. But others are involved in industrial relations besides unions and employers; thus Barbash defines it as 'the area of study and practice concerned with the employment function in modern public and private enterprise; this function involves workers, unions, managers, government and the various "publics" '.[16] Both Flanders and Dunlop write of the industrial relations *system*. Flanders emphasizes that it is a system of rules which appear in different guises: in legislation and statutory orders; in trade union regulations; in collective agreements and arbitration awards; in social conventions; in managerial decisions; and in accepted 'custom and practice'.[17] Dunlop notes that the concept of an industrial relations system is variable in scope; it may be used to characterize an immediate work place, an enterprise, a sector, or a country as a whole.[18]

[15] D. C. Miller and W. H. Form, *Industrial Sociology*, New York: Harper and Row, 1963, p. 393f.

[16] J. Barbash, 'The Elements of Industrial Relations', *British Journal of Industrial Relations*, Mar. 1964.

[17] A. Flanders, *Industrial Relations*, London: Faber, 1965, p. 10.

[18] J. T. Dunlop, *Industrial Relations Systems*, New York: Holt, 1958, p. 385.

It is difficult to remain dispassionate about industrial relations because conflicting interest groups and policies are involved. Experts sympathetic to the problems of management or trade unions naturally write from different perspectives, and their conclusions and proposals may be judged accordingly. As sociologists we need to look for theories which account for all the facts of social situations which includes understanding the motivations of different groups. What is required is a theoretical approach to industrial relations which treats the firm as a plural society rather than as an organic unity. Thus Dubin maintains that union-management relations involve conflicting goals whose differences have to be mediated through a continuous process of interaction (collective bargaining).[19] It is a power relationship: success for either management or union depends on maintaining or gaining control over decisions that affect their separate goals. Fox argues that an understanding of industrial relations must be based on a view of the firm as a pluralistic system, or a coalition of interests, rather than as a unitary system whose 'natural' pursuit of common purpose is wilfully disrupted by trade unionism.[20]

Industrial Conflict

We are concerned here with the industrial behaviour which culminates in strikes, and with the type of social structure in which this behaviour characteristically takes place. If we accept the 'plural society' or power-group interaction approach to the study of industrial relations, we may regard some form of conflict as endemic in industrial behaviour, and the question then becomes one of what constitute the form, circumstances and resolution of a particular instance.

To understand the role of strikes in industry we need to consider them as examples of open group conflict. A. Kornhauser and his associates describe the functions of open group conflict as (1) rallying the groups in conflict around a specific goal (2) bringing issues into the open and thus subjecting them to public opinion and possible social control (3) forcing a rapid resolution of the issue, and (4) stabilizing the social structure by clarifying the identity of the power-holding groups.[21] The first three of these functions seem fairly clear—

[19] R. Dubin, *Working Union-Management Relations*, Englewood Cliffs: Prentice-Hall, 1958, p. 141.

[20] A. Fox, *Industrial Sociology and Industrial Relations*, (Research Papers 3 for the Royal Commission on Trade Unions and Employers' Associations), London: HMSO, 1966.

[21] A. Kornhauser *et al.* (eds.), *Industrial Conflict*, New York: McGraw-Hill, 1954.

the first two correspond to the interests of the workers and the community respectively, while the third is usually in the interests of all involved. A theory of conflict must also enable something to be said about the circumstances which cause it to vary in intensity. Dubin suggests that it is likely to be at a maximum when the power disparity between the contending parties is in the middle range.[22] If there is power parity, the weapon of conflict is neutralized, since bargaining can take place; if there is too great power disparity, the weaker side will not provoke the stronger.

Strikes are only one way in which industrial discontent is expressed. A decline in the number of strikes does not necessarily mean that discontent is less—it may merely mean that discontent is finding expression in other ways or is not finding expression at all. The decline of the strike as one form of conflict activity is not to be taken as a sign of the removal of the conflict situation itself. Abstention from strikes is typically accompanied by emphasis on political activity, social legislation, and central economic planning as alternatives to sectional labour-management conflict. Also the introduction of automation makes strikes more difficult to conduct because it facilitates continued operation of a plant during a dispute by 'nonbargaining-unit' personnel.[23]

An excellent analysis of industrial relations in coal-mining is given by Scott and his colleagues, in which strikes are treated as part of industrial conflict.[24] Their findings contradict the commonly-held assumption that conflict in industry is necessarily harmful or always associated with inefficiency. They analyse conflict into two types and two ways in which it is expressed. *Basic* conflict exists when a group feels that its share in rewards is unjust from a long-term point of view; *procedural* conflict arises from disagreements about short-term variations in rewards and conditions of work. Also, conflict is expressed either in an organized or an unorganized way, the organized way being a group reaction to the vagaries of the industrial situation, and the unorganized way being a personal reaction to the frustrations of the industrial situation. The higher status groups more often engage in organized conflict. This analysis of types of conflict and their ways of expression promises to be applicable to studies of other industries and hence to contribute to the sociology of industrial relations.

[22] R. Dubin, 'A Theory of Conflict and Power in Union-Management Relations', *Industrial and Labor Relations Review*, July 1960.

[23] J. L. Stern, 'Automation—End of a New Day in Unionism?', *Daedalus*, Nov. 1963.

[24] W. H. Scott *et al.*, *Coal and Conflict*, Liverpool: University Press, 1963.

Eldridge and Cameron consider the differences between official and unofficial strikes.[25] They note that the dividing line is sometimes difficult to draw—for example, union officials have been known to suggest to shop stewards that unofficial action would be of assistance in their official negotiations. To incorporate unofficial strikes into a more general theory of industrial conflict, they may be seen as (a) an expression of dissatisfaction with complex rules (b) an anarchical protest that there should be rules at all (c) a protest that some other groups have broken existing rules, or (d) to point to existing anomalies in the rules and to demand reforms. In calling an unofficial strike the shop floor leader may be expressing a mood, a temper, which is not his alone but a response by a work group to their environment. He may be removed but the mood and the environment remain.

INDUSTRIAL PARTICIPATION

Industrial Democracy

'Participation' is in some ways the middle one of three concepts. At its highest level of generality, industrial democracy may be compared with political ideology; at the middle level, there are the generalized objectives sought in the name of the ideology; and at the lowest level there are the particular arrangements for workers' participation in industry.

According to Scott, industrial democracy implies the participation, to a greater or lesser extent, of all those who work in industry in determining the conditions of their working lives.[26] If 'participation' is not too narrowly defined, a growth of industrial democracy can be seen. Dahrendorf outlines five elements in this: (1) the greater organization of conflicting interest groups (2) the establishment of 'parliamentary' negotiating bodies in which these groups meet (3) the institutions of mediation and arbitration (4) formal representation of labour within the individual enterprise, and (5) tendencies towards an institutionalization of workers' participation in industrial management.[27] This last point is probably the most important in realizing the ideals of industrial democracy and the one which has been least implemented.

[25] J. Eldridge and G. Cameron, 'Unofficial Strikes: Some Objections Considered', *British Journal of Sociology*, Mar. 1964.

[26] W. H. Scott, *Industrial Democracy*, Liverpool: University Press, 1955, p. 7. see also H. A. Clegg, *A New Approach to Industrial Democracy*, Oxford: Blackwell, 1960, p. 3.

[27] R. Dahrendorf, *Class and Class Conflict in an Industrial Society*, London: Routledge, 1959, p. 257.

Forms of Participation

Ross distinguishes two aspects of control of a firm: government and management.[28] The government function is concerned with establishing and reviewing the general objects, rules and principles on which the firm is founded and securing conformity with these. The management function is involved in the executive decisions of the firm's business operations. 'In the democratic firm, government in this sense must be exercised by the members (i.e. the contributors of labour and capital) through a representative body. Given this type of government, democracy does not require that executive managers share their responsibilities with subordinates, although both democracy and efficiency do, in general, require managers to exercise their powers after consultation with those concerned.'

Workers' participation in management is fairly limited in Britain, as compared with such countries as West Germany and Yugoslavia. This is partly explained by the development of the role of trade unions in collective bargaining. Rank and file apathy in regard to union affairs is paralleled by apathy in regard to industrial participation, leaving many of the decisions which affect the interests of workers to a minority of officials or activists. Banks has investigated the type of worker who tends to be in this minority, as defined by an interest in becoming a joint consultation representative or shop steward and in being promoted to supervisor.[29] Those who were most interested in such participation had longer service with the firm, a greater knowledge and experience of its processes, and had jobs involving skill, responsibility and mental requirements generally.

One form of participation by employees in British industry is joint consultation. According to Richardson, 'consultation ranges from informal talks with the individual workers during the course of the day's work, through systems by which representatives of the workers, sometimes shop stewards, can put their point of view before the management from time to time, to regular formal representative meetings of works councils and joint production committees.'[30] But joint consultation has on the whole tended to be consultation at the workplace rather than near the boardroom. A lot depends on the attitude of management who have it within their power to initiate consultation arrangements. A study by the National Institute of Industrial Psycho-

[28] N. Ross, *The Democratic Firm*, London: Fabian Society, 1964, p. 23–4; see also W. Brown, *Exploration in Management*, London: Heinemann, 1960.

[29] J. A. Banks, *Industrial Participation*, Liverpool: University Press, 1963.

[30] J. H. Richardson, *An Introduction to the Study of Industrial Relations*, London: Allen and Unwin, 1956, p. 121.

logy showed that the more progressive managers do not look on joint consultation as primarily something which should take place only at intervals, but as a process which should be going on all the time throughout the organization.[31]

Where formal joint consultation is successful this is generally in large companies. But the weaknesses of the procedure are that joint consultation committees are often by-passed by the employer 'clearing' a decision directly with the union, centralized decision-making which frustrates local representatives, and management resentment of the new authority of the unions. In short, the majority of managements do not fully accept and practise formal consultation and all that it implies, but use it rather as a forum for company pronouncements and the airing of employee irritants.

The point has already been made that the growth of workers' participation in management has been limited by the alternative development of collective bargaining, that is, the joint formulation by management and unions of rules governing the enterprise. It is possible to argue, as does Clegg,[32] that collective bargaining is a mechanism for the protection of interests and rights and that this is the first requirement of any system of democracy. From the trade union point of view, joint consultation may be seen as little more than a sometimes useful adjunct of collective bargaining. In the absence of any widespread desire on the part of workers to participate in management, it seems that there is no effective alternative to collective bargaining as a means of protecting the interests and rights of workers in industry.

[31] National Institute of Industrial Psychology, *Joint Consultation in British Industry*, London: Staples Press, 1952.

[32] H. A. Clegg, *op. cit.*, p. 109

PART III ASPECTS OF OCCUPATIONS

12

The Labour Force and Mobility

In this third and final part of the book we turn to an area which is sometimes described as the sociology of work and occupations. The essential concern is with the social roles which individuals play in the industrial structure or in specific types of work organization and the implications that these roles have for them as persons. In this chapter some salient objective features of the labour force are briefly described, followed by a consideration of labour mobility and some correlates of occupational membership.

THE LABOUR FORCE

The labour force consists of three categories of people: those in paid employment, those who are registered as available for work, and those who are available for work but who are not registered as such. American labour force statistics cover all three of these categories, but British statistics cover only the first two groups.

The labour force is always a proportion of the total population. In Great Britain it now consists of about 25½ million persons out of a total population of 52 million. The proportion of the labour force in the total population is important because the balance is made up of dependants who must be economically supported by the working population. The trend during the ten years prior to 1963 was for the working population to increase slightly faster than the total population, but during the ten years from 1963 this trend is expected to be halted.[1] The forecast of trends is based on a number of assumptions and is therefore subject to a margin of error, but three factors are

[1] Ministry of Labour, *Manpower Studies No. 1: The Pattern of the Future*, London, HMSO, 1964.

likely to result in a falling proportion of working to dependent population: (1) a rising birth rate, (2) raising the school-leaving age to sixteen in 1972-3, and (3) a longer expectation of life in retirement.

One of the problems caused by an ageing population is the extent to which the community as a whole is willing to devote a larger proportion of its wealth to the growing group of 'non-producers'. One alternative is to provide employment, perhaps different from that done in the main part of working life, for those who have reached retiring age but are willing, and in some cases even eager, to continue working. Other consequences of an ageing labour force include its effect on incentives (the elderly are more concerned with security) and the possibilities of advancement for the younger.[2]

The percentage age and sex distribution of the labour force was in 1966, and is expected to be in 1971 and 1981, as follows:[3]

Age Group	1966	1971	1981
15–19	11·9	9·4	9·7
20–39	38·9	41·0	42·9
40–64	46·0	46·1	44·2
65 and over	3·2	3·4	3·3
Males	65·4	65·5	64·8
Females	34·6	34·5	35·2
Married	19·1	20·6	22·6
Others	15·5	13·9	12·7

The trend is expected to be towards an older labour force, containing a fairly stable proportion of men to women, but a greater proportion of married to single women workers.

The employment of the population is analysed in the Census and other government publications by occupation (types of skill, e.g. clerk, painter) and industry (the end to which the skill is put, e.g. insurance, building).[4] The industries which have employed increasing numbers of workers in recent years include miscellaneous services, and national and local government service. Those with slightly decreasing numbers of employees include agriculture and fishing, mining and construc-

[2] R. Dubin, *The World of Work*, Englewood Cliffs: Prentice-Hall, 1958, p. 149.

[3] 'Forecasts of the Working Population: 1966–81', *Ministry of Labour Gazette*, Nov. 1966.

[4] Detailed figures on employment by occupation and industry are given in the official Census tables and on industry periodically in the monthly *Employment and Productivity Gazette*.

tion.[5] There has been a steady rise in the numbers employed in white-collar and service occupations, especially those concerned with health and education.

There is a tendency for the length of the working week to decline in most industries, and soon the 40-hour *official* working week may become the general standard. But overtime working has been increasing. Although normal hours of work per week fell between 1958 and 1962 from 44·5 to 42·4, the actual hours worked fell only from 47·8 to 47;1.[6] Overtime working is not only financially advantageous to the worker, who generally prefers more income to shorter hours, but may also be technically advantageous to the employer, in that costly plant can be more fully used. The effects of shift work on the non-work life of employees have been studied both in Britain and America; the general conclusion seems to be that most people can adjust physically to shift work over a period, but that the social and psychological effects constitute a more serious problem.[7]

The problem of the integration of immigrants, and particularly of coloured workers, into the labour force has grown in significance with the increase of immigration in recent years. Some employers claim to accept anyone who is qualified to do the job irrespective of colour, while in other industries (particularly those involving contact with customers) a covert colour bar is operated. Both managements and unions have been criticized for practising racial discrimination. However, some employers, especially those who find it difficult to attract labour, are coming increasingly to depend on the recruitment of coloured workers, for example, London Transport, hospitals, building, road-sweeping, and certain factories.[8]

Although detailed consideration of amounts and methods of payment for work is strictly outside the scope of our subject, one development is of special sociological interest. During the last two decades 'fringe benefits' as a proportion of workers' total income have risen steeply.[9] These include paid non-working time, family allowances paid by the employer, factory clinics, life insurance, profit-sharing, interest-

[5] Decreasing numbers of employees are not necessarily associated with decreasing output; a smaller labour force may use more efficient methods and machines to raise output.

[6] E. G. Whybrew, 'Overtime and the Reduction of the Working Week', *British Journal of Industrial Relations*, July 1964.

[7] F. P. Cook, *Shift Work*, London: Institute of Personnel Management, 1954; P. L. Mott *et al.*, Shift Work, Ann Arbor; University of Michigan Press, 1965.

[8] R. B. Davison, 'Immigration and Unemployment in the UK, 1955-1962', *British Journal of Industrial Relations*, Feb. 1963.

[9] A. Rubner, *Fringe Benefits*, London: Putnam, 1962.

free loans, payment for transport costs, meals at work, company housing, and so on. Not all employees, of course, share in these benefits, and the main recipients tend to be in industries where there is a shortage of labour or in circumstances where the employer would find it difficult to replace employees with certain skills or expertise.

OCCUPATIONAL MOBILITY

Occupational or labour mobility refers generally to the movement of workers. This movement can be of six types: (1) in or out of the labour force (2) changes in the content of the job (3) changes in the employer (4) changes in the occupation or skills used (5) changes in the industry or ends to which skills are put, and (6) changes in the geographical place of work.[10] Quite often one kind of change involves another. Occupational mobility is also sometimes used to describe a comparison of father's and son's occupation (inter-generational mobility) and in this sense it is an important factor in social mobility.

In the post-war period there have been two large-scale British surveys of labour mobility. The first covered the period 1945–1949 and involved over 5,000 men and women.[11] It was found that 28% of the men and 32% of the women had changed their employer at least once during this period; more young than old had changed their jobs, more manual than non-manual, and more unskilled than skilled. There were also differences in mobility rates among industries, for example, the rate was nearly twice as high in building as in miscellaneous services.

Over a lifetime men had made on average nearly four and women three changes of occupation, industry, or location. Of the men's changes, roughly two were of occupation or industry within the same town, one was of occupation or industry involving a move, and one was geographical only (including those in the armed forces). Occupational changes were analysed according to whether or not they were within the same broad group of occupations. Among the findings were that 61% of changes by those in professional or technical occupations were within that group, but only 30% of clerical workers' changes were within clerical work. Only 1% of operatives moved into professional or technical jobs, but 10% of the latter changed to the

[10] P. M. Hauser, 'Mobility in Labour Force Participation', in E. W. Bakke *et al.*, *Labour Mobility and Economic Opportunity*, New York: Technology Press, 1954, p. 11.

[11] G. Thomas, *Labour Mobility in Great Britain, 1945–1949*, London: Government Social Survey, 1949.

former. Most people changing their jobs went from one industry to another, though they often stayed within the same broad group, for example, manufacturing industry. In short, workers appear to be more tied by their occupation than by the industry in which they work.

The second labour mobility survey was carried out in 1963, covering the previous ten years and involving a sample of nearly 20,000 men and women.[12] It was found that 57% of those who had been in the labour force in those ten years had remained in the same job, 19% had changed jobs once and 11% twice in the period. About 1% had at least ten jobs in the ten years. Persons of managerial and executive status changed jobs less frequently than those in other occupational status groups. An analysis of reasons for leaving jobs showed that roughly one-fifth represented non-voluntary terminations or retirements, another fifth moved for better pay or prospects, and a similar proportion terminated through ill-health or changes in domestic responsibility. Further research was planned to forecast the future pattern of occupational change, so that action could be taken in advance to provide retraining where redeployment was likely to be necessary, and to identify skills for which future demands might arise.

In measuring inter-generational mobility, the father's occupation is usually cross-classified by the son's. For example, if 60% of the sons of professional fathers are professionals (40% mobile), while 20% of the sons of clerks are clerks (80% mobile), the latter are said to be twice as mobile as the former.[13] But this measure does not take into account the number of positions available in each occupational class. If, for example, there are three times more unskilled workers than professionals then we should expect three times more mobility into unskilled work than into professional. Total mobility is the result of structural or availability factors plus personal or group factors. We must therefore ask whether movement within the occupational structure is more restricted for some groups than for others, since it is a question of share of opportunities.

It is difficult to interpret changes in the rate of occupational mobility. In general, it seems that they can mostly be explained by changes in the occupational structure. The proportion of white-collar workers is increasing and that of agricultural and unskilled workers decreasing. More people are needed in administration work, especially to run the expanding social and welfare services. These changes have

[12] 'Mobility Between Industries and Jobs', *Ministry of Labour Gazette*, July 1966.

[13] N. Rogoff, *Recent Trends in Occupational Mobility*, Glencoe: Free Press, 1953, p. 29.

combined to result in apparent 'upward' mobility. A second factor is that of differential fertility—the tendency of the wealthier to have fewer children. Because families of higher occupational status have generally had less than their proportionate share of children, room is left for others to rise into that status.

We may briefly consider some factors which influence occupational mobility. The state of the labour market plays a big part. Voluntary movement is slight when job opportunities are few, and when opportunities are greater differentials in earnings and fringe benefits become more important in explaining mobility. Wilensky has noted the effect of type of employing organization.[14] Those in organizations with 'tall' hierarchies (affording careers with many stages) and with a high ratio of managers to managed are more likely to experience mobility than those in organizations with a long, prescribed training period. Broom and Smith have coined the term 'bridging occupation' to describe an occupation which provides, through work experience, the conditions and opportunities for movement from one to another.[15] Attributes of those in bridging occupations were listed as: resocialization (redirection of the perspectives and aspirations of the occupant), independency, health and physical bearing, access to information or to individuals in influential or useful positions, and financial competence. Examples given of bridging occupations were servants, soldiers, school teachers, and those in occupations connected with mass communication and entertainment.

The present writer has put forward the concept of 'retrospective bridging' in connection with those occupations in which experience of other kinds of work is relatively frequent and comparatively highly valued.[16] Using survey data, three different types of occupations were examined for the degree to which their members had been occupationally mobile, and some of the characteristics of mobile and non-mobile individuals were noted.

CORRELATES OF OCCUPATIONAL MEMBERSHIP

For much evidence of correlates of occupational membership, we have to rely on social class data rather than specifically occupational data.

[14] H. L. Wilensky, 'Work, Careers and Social Integration', *International Social Science Journal*, No. 4, 1960.

[15] L. Broom and J. H. Smith, 'Bridging Occupations', *British Journal of Sociology*, Dec. 1963.

[16] S. R. Parker, 'Retrospective "Bridging" of Three Occupational Groups', *Sociology*, Jan. 1967.

Even research on the latter is very limited in Britain, though findings in other countries suggest testable hypotheses. In Chicago in 1940 a person from the lowest economic class could expect to live five years less than average and ten years less than those in the highest economic class;[17] such differences are probably decreasing to the extent that primary poverty is diminished. Infant death rates in France in 1954 varied by occupation of the father from 1·7 per 100 of those in the medical profession to 8·6 per 100 of miners; the difference was due only partly to low income, since ignorance and inattention were also factors.[18]

Suicide rates are generally higher for white-collar and professional groups than for manual workers, but there are significant differences within these broad occupational groups which reflect particular work experiences. Lonely occupations, such as domestic service and lodging-house keeping, have high suicide rates, while occupations which bring men into close contact with each other, such as miners and the clergy, have low suicide rates.[19] Concerning mental health generally, American evidence shows that neurosis is concentrated in higher classes and psychosis in the lower, and that there are differences in diagnosis and methods of treatment between members of different classes with the same disorder.[20]

One of the most interesting and complex correlates of occupational membership is that of social conformity. High status occupations include those giving personal freedom and a degree of immunity from moral sanctions.[21] But occupations associated with 'sacred elements' or charged with social responsibility require their practitioners to function as models or examples. These two points mean that the strictest control over non-work behaviour tends to be found in occupations with important role-setting obligations, identification with sacred symbols, and relatively low status. Those occupations with least control over non-work behaviour tend to have high status and no involvement with sacred elements. Teaching is an example of relatively strict control over non-work behaviour, and advertising of relatively little control.

[17] E. V. Schneider, *Industrial Sociology*, New York: McGraw-Hill, 1957, p. 382.

[18] N. Anderson, *The Urban Community*, London: Routledge, 1960, p. 144.

[19] W. L. Tonge, 'Loneliness, Sexual Difficulties and Guilt', in C. Varah (ed.), *The Samaritans*, London: Constable, 1965, p. 128.

[20] A. B. Hollingshead and F. Redlich, *Social Class and Mental Illness*, New York: Wiley, 1958.

[21] T. Caplow, *The Sociology of Work*, Minneapolis: University of Minnesota Press, 1954, pp. 129–30.

OCCUPATIONAL ROLES

The scope and pervasiveness of occupational roles are important aspects of the sociology of occupations. The concept of *role* denotes the recognized part played by an individual in a social organization, and structure clusters of roles constitute one feature of social organization. The *scope* of an occupational role refers to the part that the incumbent plays in the work organization; while the *pervasiveness* of an occupational role indicates its degree of penetration into other life-roles. The higher the status of an occupation, the more numerous and specific its role elements tend to be.[22] Thus only a few requirements for the position of floor sweeper are imposed, since this occupation involves only some limited, well-defined central elements and virtually no peripheral elements; whereas the position of an executive in a large company requires many more qualities than those of formal competence.

The pervasiveness of an occupational role bears no direct relation to its status. Some highly pervasive occupations, such as that of village policeman, carry relatively low status (though often high *prestige*) while less pervasive occupations, such as that of industrialist, are accorded high status. Banton spells out the difference between more and less pervasive occupational roles, though his example of blacksmith might be replaced by almost anyone who has a 'nine-to-five' job over which there is relatively lax social control: '... blacksmith is a role which someone assumes for part of the day only; when he has finished work the incumbent is not expected to behave in any way different from people who are not blacksmiths.'[23] This role is contrasted with that of the policeman, who has obligations he is supposed never to lay aside. Being a policeman usually comes to affect a man's whole outlook on life.

Some occupational roles, because of the element of service to others which they involve, tend to pervade the rest of life. Social workers in general, and residential social workers in particular, may find it neither easy nor appropriate to stop being of service to others in their off-duty hours.[24] Another example of a pervasive occupational role is that of

[22] S. A. Weinstock, 'Role Elements: A Link Between Acculturation and Occupational Status', *British Journal of Sociology*, June 1963.

[23] M. Banton, *Roles: An Introduction to the Study of Social Relations*, London: Tavistock, 1965, p. 40.

[24] For example, mental welfare and child care officers tend more than people in business occupations to let their work encroach relatively greatly on their free time (S. R. Parker, 'Type of Work, Friendship Patterns and Leisure', *Human Relations*, Aug. 1964).

the lawyer, who often assumes extra-professional or citizenship obligations. This is because there are 'behaviour expectations pertaining to the lawyer in relation to his community and society which are not those of every citizen and which are not part of the technical function of the lawyer.'[25]

[25] W. I. Wardwell and A. L. Wood, 'The Extra Professional Role the of Lawyer', *American Journal of Sociology*, Jan. 1956.

13

The Subjective Experience of Work

AFTER considering some of the 'objective' features of occupational membership and roles, we now turn to more 'subjective' aspects of occupational experience. There are a number of concepts which are relevant here, and our first task is to try to define them in relation to each other and to see to what extent different terms are used in the same or very similar senses. There are two broad groups of concepts: those relating to the evaluation of work as a social activity or institution, and those relating to the subjective experience of particular work roles.

The first group consists of two concepts, ideology and value. A work *ideology* is held by the members of a society generally or by a particular social group and refers to a clustering of lower-order concepts such as values, attitudes, beliefs and opinions. It attaches to work behaviour and institutions in the most general sense, and sometimes the term 'ethos' is used to denote something very similar to ideology. Work *values* are more specific 'conceptions of the desirable'[1] by which a particular society or group judges features of work to be good or bad. The differences between these two concepts should become clear as we examine research involving them in the sections below.

The group of concepts referring to the subjective experience of work roles includes, from the more general to the less, attitudes (or orientation), involvement, motivation, and satisfaction. There is a link between attitudes and values in that a work *attitude* describes the general approach that a person has to his work as a result of accepting or rejecting certain values of his society or group. Work *involvement* refers to a special class of attitudes and signifies the degree to which a person is identified psychologically with his work or the importance

[1] C. Kluckhohn, 'Values and Value-Orientations in The Theory of Action', in T. Parsons and E. Shils, *Toward a General Theory of Action*, Cambridge Mass.: Harvard University Press, 1951, p. 422.

of work in his total self-image.[2] The meaning of work to a person is another way of indicating the quality of his involvement in it. *Motivation* usually refers to a specific job or narrow range of jobs rather than to work in general and constitutes the factors that pull people towards achieving certain goals through the work. Finally, *satisfaction*, which is also normally job-specific, is a function of the discrepancy between what a worker expects, or thinks he should get, and what he actually experiences in the work situation.

WORK IDEOLOGY

Although the concept of ideology was used originally in connection with the theory of ideas, it became a specific formulation and ultimately, in Marxist thought, to denote an interest in a sociological analysis of an opponent's ideas. Mannheim incorporated ideology into his studies of the sociology of knowledge and held that the ideas, values and attitudes of a given group are embedded in the social conditions under which the group lives. From such an approach one would expect that, if occupational groups have conditions which differentiate them meaningfully from other occupational groups, they would also develop differing ideologies.

However, the remarkable thing about ideologies in the modern industrial world is not their divergence but their convergence. While differences between classes and occupational groups may emerge at the level of values,[3] there is general consensus at the level of ideology. Bendix has shown that a 'managerial ideology' has developed which serves to justify the power of management in terms of basic cultural values;[4] further, this ideology characterizes not just the business community but virtually the total American society. Both in Britain and America there is no evidence of a deep or permanent ideological conflict between opposing interest groups in regard to national economic and social policies. Indeed, it may be argued that 'ideology', in the sense of a comprehensive system of ideas, is too strong a word to use in connection with social thought in Britain and America, and

[2] T. M. Lodahl, 'Patterns of Job Attitudes in Two Assembly Technologies', *Administrative Science Quarterly*, Dec. 1963.

[3] For a description of middle- and working-class values see A. Cohen, *Delinquent Boys*, London: Routledge, 1956, pp. 88–91, 96–7; see also H. H. Hyman, 'The Value Systems of Different Classes', in R. Bendix and S. Lipset (eds.), *Class, Status and Power*, Glencoe: Free Press, 1953.

[4] R. Bendix, *Work and Authority in Industry*, New York: Wiley, 1957.

that some such term as 'shared understandings' would better describe the situation.[5]

Sometimes the concept of ideology is used in a narrower sense than the above, as when describing an occupational rather than a work ideology. Thus Dibble has described the relationship between occupational ideologies and other systems of belief.[6] He examined the conditions under which occupational ideologies will or will not be diffused beyond the groups in which they are first espoused. Mack has suggested that the type of occupational ideology varies according to the determinateness of the occupational role, that is, its degree of flexibility in role expectations.[7] People in occupations with indeterminate roles tend to be means-oriented and to view work instrumentally; those in occupations with determinate roles tend to view work as an end and to define life goals in ocupational terms.

WORK VALUES

Much of the research on work values has been concerned with the ways in which they are internalized during the process of occupational choice and training. One of the most comprehensive and theoretically enlightened studies is that of Rosenberg and his associates.[8] They gathered data on a nationwide basis of American students' preferences, expectations and aspirations in the work sphere. In general, students were found to fall into three groups: those who ask what rewards they will get from their work; those who ask whether it will be a challenging, creative experience; and those who ask whether they will enjoy working with the people. Students planning to enter different occupations exhibited these values in varying proportions; for example, 'people-oriented' values were most strongly stressed by students planning to enter social work, medicine, social science and personnel work. Thus the relationship between occupational values and the nature of the work suggests that what the student wants from his work delimits and channels the range of occupations in which he might become interested. Several other investigators have examined the

[5] C. Kerr in an introduction to *ibid.*, p. xii.

[6] V. K. Dibble, 'Occupations and Ideologies', *American Journal of Sociology*, Sept. 1962.

[7] R. W. Mack, 'Occupational Ideology and the Determinate Role', *Social Forces*, Oct. 1957.

[8] M. Rosenberg *et al.*, *Occupations and Values*, Glencoe: Free Press, 1957.

relationship between values and prospective careers, including the development of identification with an occupation.[9]

Moving to the level of the occupational world itself, Lyman compared the two broad groups of white-collar and blue-collar workers for differences in values attached to work.[10] She concluded that the former emphasized the nature of the work itself and freedom, and the latter the physically easy nature of the work, the economic rewards, conditions of work and cleanliness. These differences were not a function of differences in job satisfaction, for when satisfaction was held constant a pattern of different reasons for liking or disliking jobs was found. However, she noted the difficulty that the results might be open to other interpretations than value differences, for example, differences in what is taken for granted.

An example of different value orientations of two groups of employees doing roughly the same kind of tasks is given by Boggs.[11] Laboratory workers were divided into professionals and technicians, largely on the basis of education and prestige. It was found that the professionals were far more likely to say that the kind of work they did was the most important thing about a life's work, while the technicians more often said that security or pay was the most important thing. One explanation of this difference in values is that the professionals expected to participate more fully in all phases of their work and were often rewarded socially for doing so.

WORK ATTITUDES

Work attitudes describe the general approach that people take to their work as a result of having certain values. In this context the term 'orientation' means much the same as attitude, that is, a readiness to respond to aspects of work in terms of the values held. There have been many studies of the attitudes of people in various occupations and work situations. The findings of such studies may be grouped according to a small number of significant variables. The manual-nonmanual categories, levels of skill, and age groups are obvious examples, though

[9] S. Box and S. Cotgrove, 'Scientific Identity, Occupational Selection and Role Strain', *British Journal of Sociology*, March 1966; R. L. and I. L. Simpson, 'Values, Personal Influence and Occupational Choice', *Social Forces*, Dec. 1960; H. S. Becker and J. W. Carper, 'The Development of Identification with an Occupation', *American Journal of Sociology*, Jan. 1956.

[10] E. Lyman, 'Occupational Differences and Values Attached to Work', *American Journal of Sociology*, Jan. 1956.

[11] S. T. Boggs, 'The Values of Laboratory Workers', *Human Organization*, Fall 1963.

work situation variables such as degree of autonomy and social interaction are also important. To illustrate briefly some consequences of these variables for work attitudes we may select four groups of occupations which together account for a large proportion of the labour force: professionals, clerks, skilled craftsmen, and semi-skilled factory workers.

Caplow notes a number of features of professional work which combine to produce typical attitudes.[12] These features are: the distinction drawn between co-professionals and laymen, the concentration of interest which marks the professional career, the long period of training, and informal association outside working hours. The professional attitude to work is often contrasted with the bureaucratic attitude. The former is characteristic of the 'cosmopolitan', who tends to have a relatively low loyalty to his employing organization, a high commitment to his role skills and an 'outgroup' reference; while the bureaucrat typically shows high loyalty to his employing organization, low commitment to role skills and an 'ingroup' reference.[13]

The work attitudes of clerks reflect their varied work situations and social class affiliations. As Lockwood has shown, the older, paternalistic work relations and environment of the clerk precluded any sense of identification with other types of worker, and led to individualistic aspirations to advancement akin to those of professionals.[14] But as office units have become larger and working relationships and techniques more impersonal and standardized—in short, more like those of the factory—group feeling, collective action and a 'trade union' attitude to earnings and working conditions have developed among clerks.

As a representative of skilled craft occupations we may take the printer. Studies in both Britain and America have described the nature of the 'occupational community' in which printers tend to live. Lipset and his associates suggest that intrinsic interest in the craft tends to promote a high degree of participation in the work organization and particularly in union activities.[15] In this country, Cannon has analysed the factors which promote occupational community (chiefly the need for help of other printers in doing certain work-tasks, and their status and isolation within the firm), and has described how the

[12] T. Caplow, *The Sociology of Work*, Minneapolis: University of Minnesota Press, 1954, p. 131f.

[13] A. W. Gouldner, 'Cosmopolitans and Locals', *Administrative Science Quarterly*, Dec. 1957.

[14] D. Lockwood, *The Blackcoated Worker*, London: Allen and Unwin, 1958.

[15] S. M. Lipset *et al.*, *Union Democracy*, Glencoe: Free Press, 1956.

influence of this community extends to inducing conformity to moral values and norms of behaviour.[16]

The fourth group whose work attitudes we may briefly consider are semi-skilled factory workers. Car assembly workers have been the subject of several studies both in Britain and America, and may serve as an example of research which could be carried out on those in other occupations. Blauner has summarized the findings of previous attitude research on 'the man on the track': he 'approaches the classic model of the self-estranged worker'; he is 'the blue-collar prototype of "the mass man in mass society" ' and often he is 'the prototype of the militant worker as well.'[17] Goldthorpe's findings from his study of car workers at Luton broadly confirm this 'image', but he suggests that too little attention has been paid to the prior orientations which workers have towards employment, and which in turn influence their choice of job, the meaning they give to work and their definition of the work situation.[18]

In addition to prior orientations and those generated by participation in a certain kind of work situation, attitudes are also influenced by status position within a work organization. Thus Lieberman has noted the effect of role changes on attitudes. Workers who were made foremen became more favourable to management (though if demoted they reverted to worker attitudes), while those who were made shop stewards became more favourable to the union.[19]

WORK INVOLVEMENT

We commonly speak of someone as 'involved' in his work if he makes a considerable emotional investment in it—if it 'means a lot to him'. But involvement in that sense is only quantitative, and says nothing about possible different *types*. Involvement may be seen to have three aspects: the meaning that is attached to work, the feeling of identification with or alienation from work and its objects, and the degree to which work is a central life interest. We shall consider each of these aspects in turn.

Psychologists are familiar with the notion that the nature and set-

[16] I. C. Cannon, *The Social Situation of the Skilled Worker*, University of London Ph.D. thesis, 1961.

[17] R. Blauner, *Alienation and Freedom*, Chicago University Press, 1964.

[18] J. H. Goldthorpe, 'Attitudes and Behaviour of Car Assembly Workers', *British Journal of Sociology*, Sept. 1966. See also the later books by Goldthorpe *et al.* in the series *The Affluent Worker* (on industrial attitudes, political attitudes, and class structure), Cambridge Univ. Press, 1968-9.

[19] S. Liebermann, 'The Effects of Change in Roles on the Attitudes of Role Occupants', *Human Relations*, Nov. 1956.

ting of a man's work has a special meaning for him as an individual, that it is part and parcel of his whole philosophy. Sociologists are concerned with the meaning held by 'typical persons', that is, individuals subject to similar environmental (material and social) conditions. A number of studies have sought to define various meanings of work held by people in different occupations or work situations. Weiss and Kahn found that over three-fourths of respondents defined work either as activity which was necessary though not enjoyed or as activity which was scheduled or paid for.[20] The first definition was associated with occupations which permit some autonomy (professionals and salespeople), and the second with occupations affording neither autonomy nor social standing (factory workers and labourers).

Friedmann and Havighurst compared the meaning of work to five occupational groups.[21] The workers of lower skill and socio-economic status were more likely to see their work as having no other meaning than that of earning money. Coalminers had a more personal sense than steelworkers of being pitted against their environment, and expressed feelings of accomplishment and pride at having conquered it. Skilled craftsmen showed a very high degree of emphasis on work as a source of self-respect and the respect of others. Salespeople attached many extra-economic meanings to their work, and even routine and association with others became meaningful life-experiences for them. Finally, the physicians were found to stress most the public service aspects of their jobs.

The method used by Morse and Weiss to study the meaning of work was to ask questions on the hypothesis that the economic necessity for their informants to work was removed.[22] They concluded that to those in middle-class occupations work means having something interesting to do, having a chance to accomplish things, and to contribute. By contrast, those in working-class occupations view work as synonymous with activity. These differences in work meanings correspond to differences in the content of the jobs. The content of professional, managerial and sales jobs concerns symbols and the handling of 'cases', and so a life without such work would be less purposeful, stimulating and challenging. Working-class occupations emphasize working with tools and machines, and the individual is oriented to

[20] R. S. Weiss and R. L. Kahn, 'Definitions of Work and Occupations', *Social Problems*, Fall 1960.

[21] E. A. Friedmann and R. J. Havighurst, *The Meaning of Work and Retirement*, Chicago University Press, 1954, pp. 3–5, 173–8.

[22] N. Morse and R. Weiss, 'The Function and Meaning of Work and the Job', *American Sociological Review*, April 1955.

the effort rather than to the end—life without work would mean life without anything to do.

The theme of alienation from work, although originally part of the Marxist critique of the division of labour in capitalist society, is today widely used to describe the disengagement of self from the occupational role. Frustrated by the lack of meaning in the tasks alloted to him and by the impersonality of his role in the work organization, the alienated worker turns to non-work life for values and identity: 'I only work here, but if you want to know me as I really am, come to my home and meet my family.'[23] Alienation can also take subtler forms among professionals and executives, for whom it may be fashionable to be cynical about one's work but quite 'satisfied' with one's job.

Experience of alienation is not confined to a few special occupations, though it tends to be associated with certain characteristic work situations. In large-scale bureaucracies it is apparent in the administration of men as if they were things.[24] In an automated factory or office it takes the form of increasing the number of people who deal with the world through abstractions. As Walker puts it, '... we are moving from a working world still heavily coloured and characterized by immediate sensory experience to one dominated by a multitude of categories and abstractions.'[25]

An important contribution to understanding the nature and correlates of alienation from work has recently been made by Blauner.[26] In making a comparative analysis of four types of work situation he demonstrates convincingly that alienation is a function of the type of industry in which people work. He analysed the dimensions of alienation as *powerlessness* (inability to control the work process), *meaninglessness* (inability to develop a sense of purpose connecting the job to the overall productive process), *isolation* (inability to belong to integrated industrial communities), and *self-estrangement* (failure to become involved in the activity of work as a mode of self-expression). The four types of industry compared were printing, textiles, automobile and chemical. The general picture was of a relative lack of alienation in craft printing, an increase in machine textiles, a further increase in the assembly-line automobile industry, but a

[23] P. L. Berger, 'Some General Observations on the Problem of Work', in P. L. Berger (ed.), *The Human Shape of Work*, New York: Macmillan, 1964, p. 217.

[24] E. Fromm, 'Freedom in the Work Situation', in M. Harrington and P. Jacobs, *Labor in a Free Society*, University of California Press, 1959.

[25] C. R. Walker, *Toward the Automatic Factory*, New Haven: Yale University Press, 1957, p. 216.

[26] R. Blauner, *op. cit.*

reduction to something like the printing level in the automated chemical industry.

A concept allied to, but in a sense the opposite of, alienation is that of *central life interest*. As used by Dubin, this refers to a significant area of social experience.[27] Assuming that social participation in a sphere may be necessary but not important to an individual, Dubin classified replies by industrial workers to a series of three-choice questions as job-oriented, non-job-oriented, or indifferent. The results showed that by a margin of three to one work was not in general a central life interest for industrial workers. Orzack gave an amended version of Dubin's schedule to a sample of professional nurses, and his results confirmed the prediction that they would be much more oriented to work as a central life interest than industrial workers.[28] The present writer also gave a battery of 'central life interest' questions to bank employees, youth employment and child care officers with the result that the first group emerged as substantially more non-work oriented than the other two.[29] This difference in central life interest was found to be associated with other work attitudes and with various work situation factors.

THE MOTIVATION TO WORK

There is a link between this section and the next on work satisfaction, in that the factors which motivate a person to work may be regarded as prospective 'satisfiers'. A good deal of research has been carried out by industrial psychologists on motives and incentives, and the results of this have been well summarized by J. A. C. Brown:[30]

(1) There is no one ideal incentive. Incentives vary from one culture to another, from one firm to another, and from one individual to another.

(2) The law of diminishing returns applies to all material incentives.

(3) Incentives may conflict with other motives (e.g. a worker may ignore financial incentives if he feels that he may work himself out of a job).

(4) Except under conditions when wages are very low or during periods of inflation, money is one of the least powerful incentives.

[27] R. Dubin 'Industrial Workers' Worlds', *Social Problems*, Jan. 1956.

[28] L. Orzack, 'Work as a "Central Life Interest" of Professionals', *Social Problems*, Fall 1959.

[29] S. R. Parker, 'Work and Non-work in Three Occupations', *Sociological Review*, March 1965.

[30] J. A. C. Brown, 'The Social Psychology of Industry', Harmondsworth: Pelican, 1954, p. 202.

(5) Motives tend to become 'monetized': people have been taught that money is the key to satisfaction, so when they feel something is wrong with their lives they naturally ask for more money.

An important study which links the concepts of motivation and satisfaction is that of Herzberg and his associates.[31] Using samples of engineers and accountants, they showed that factors which act as 'satisfiers' (and which have a definite motivational character) are different from those which cause dissatisfaction. Satisfied workers stressed achievement, recognition, the work itself, responsibility and advancement. Dissatisfied workers complained about company policy and administration, supervision, salary, interpersonal relations, and working conditions. In a further study of automobile and electronics assembly-line workers, Lodahl confirmed these findings and urged that job satisfaction, job motivation, and job involvement are on levels of increasing emotional intensity of depth. It is, however, unfortunate that he refers to the conditions that surround the work (the 'satisfiers') as the affective component and to rewards from the work itself (the 'motivators') as the instrumental component; it is more usual to describe those as 'instrumental' and 'expressive' factors respectively.

WORK SATISFACTION

There have been several hundred studies of job or work satisfaction and it is not possible to do more here than to review some of their main conclusions and to draw attention to some of their limitations.[32] Data have been obtained in a number of different ways. The most usual is simply to enquire of the informant whether and in what way he finds his present job satisfying. Sometimes the question 'in what way?' is asked in an open form, and sometimes the informant is presented with a list of factors from which to choose or to rank in order. Another method is to ask what makes a job good or bad. A more sophisticated approach is first to posit certain needs in relation to work and then to enquire about the degree to which these are actually satisfied.

Many occupations have been the subject of work satisfaction studies, though factory and office work have predominated. Among skilled factory workers and craftsmen intrinsic satisfaction with the work itself is frequently found, especially when the job involves the completion of a whole project. Assembly line workers attach more importance to

[31] F. Herzberg *et al.*, *The Motivation to Work*, New York: Wiley, 1959.

[32] This section is based on S. R. Parker, 'Work Satisfaction: A review of the Literature', Government Social Survey Methodological Paper no. 115, London, 1964, where details of sources may be found.

being able to control to some extent the pace and methods of their work. Variety of operations is a source of satisfaction to both factory and office workers, and among the latter the friendliness of the working group is often mentioned (particularly by females). In comparing proportions of satisfied workers in different occupations, there seem to be separate scales for manual and non-manual jobs, with more satisfaction found at the higher levels of skill in each group. Professional workers are most satisfied, and semi-skilled and unskilled manual workers least.

Of 'special situation' factors which influence satisfaction, social interaction seems to be most important. Autonomy in the work situation—freedom to make decisions and take responsibilities—is positively related to satisfaction. If three individuals are engaged on the same work with mates doing a better, worse, or the same job respectively, the first is likely to show least job enjoyment. Permissive supervision and leadership, and being consulted in advance about changes in work processes, are conducive to satisfaction. In general, jobs which involve dealing with people provide more satisfaction than those which do not.

Satisfaction is correlated with certain personal attributes. Women are generally more satisfied with their work than men, even when their jobs are lower in authority position, status and income. Satisfaction generally increases with age, although there is a tendency for the young to find this in intrinsic aspects of the work and the old to find it in the social and technical environment. Higher social class and status are related to satisfaction but, among those doing the same kind of work, better education is associated with lower satisfaction. Insecurity in a job, even when accompanied by good objective conditions, adversely affects satisfaction. The data on the relation of satisfaction to productivity are ambiguous: some studies have found a positive relationship, some a negative, and some no relationship.

In evaluating the conclusions of the various work satisfaction studies certain methodological criticisms need to be taken into account. Figures of general satisfaction with a job tell us very little, since we do not know what the questions mean to the people who answer them. The frame of reference of questions is often very limited, so that expressions of satisfaction are narrow and made without consciousness of possible alternative conditions. Also, we must differentiate between what people consciously think about their satisfaction and what they may feel unconsciously. The tendency to repress dissatisfaction is strongly supported by the widespread feeling that not to be satisfied is an admission of failure.

14

Work and Leisure

OUR concern in this chapter is with the relationship between the working and leisure lives of individuals occupying certain social roles. We suggest that this relationship is a *functional* one, and shall therefore focus attention on the role of leisure in life patterns rather than on the content of leisure activities.[1] After considering definitions of work and leisure, we shall discuss variables which affect the nature of their relationship, concluding with a review of the progress which has been made towards a theory of work and leisure.

THE NATURE OF WORK AND LEISURE

Although we can make certain statements about the nature of work and leisure separately, they have full sociological meaning only in relation to each other. Work is an activity that is carried on under conditions in which there are normally demands with respect to time and place and in which effort is directed to the production of goods and services.[2] In leisure-time activities, theoretically at least, the demands are self-imposed; there is some feeling of freedom and normally a contrast to the external controls of time, space and production imposed in the work situation. For a minority of persons their work is to some extent also their leisure, or perhaps they do not find it meaningful to divide their lives into these two spheres. But the fact remains that for most people in present industrial society leisure is quite clearly demarcated from work.

[1] It has proved virtually impossible to conceptualize leisure on a behavioural basis alone. See B. M. Berger, 'The Sociology of Leisure', *Industrial Relations*, Feb. 1962.

[2] J. E. Anderson, 'Psychological Aspects of the Use of Free Time', in W. Donahue *et al.* (eds.), *Free Time: Challenge to Later Maturity*, Ann Arbor: University of Michigan Press, 1958.

If work is a social demand and leisure a kind of individual demand, the same holds true for contributions. Work contributes something which others are willing to pay for (or for which others would have to be paid if one did not do it oneself), while leisure is concerned with contributing to the satisfaction of self.[3] Leisure may be regarded as an end, distinct from work as a means, provided that we make the exceptions that leisure is sometimes seen as a means to better work and that certain types of work may be valued for their own sakes. A social ethic, in fact, may be based either on work or leisure or an integration of the two. The movement which has taken place from a work-based Protestant ethic to a more leisure-based ethic does not mean that the former now exercises no influence. There is still a widespread belief that leisure is something that has to be earned and re-earned, except for the very old.[4]

It has been assumed so far that all life-space, that is, activities or ways of spending time that people have, can be classified as either work or leisure. But important differences exist *within* as well as between the categories of work and leisure that make a closer analysis necessary. On the other side of work, there is time actually spent on the job, and a fringe area which is defined according to one's conception of how far the domain of work extends. DeGrazia calls this fringe area 'work-related time', meaning time spent in order to appear at work presentably (travelling to work or grooming oneself for work) or in doing things that one would not ordinarily do if it were not for work, like the husband's doing a share of the working wife's housework.[5] Another type of fringe work area has been identified by Dumazedier and Latouche: that of *work obligation,* or work which takes place after the statutory hours of labour.[6] This includes both supplementary work in the firm and complementary work outside the firm, often outside the main occupation. It also includes that part of domestic work which is imposed by the needs of the family.

It has been suggested that free time is simply a space of time, while leisure is an activity or 'state of being'.[7] But this contrast is not confined to the area of non-work—it applies also in the work sphere. The two worlds of time and activity are not the domains of

[3] G. Soule, *Time for Living*, New York: Viking Press, 1955, p. 124.

[4] M. Mead, 'The Pattern of Leisure in Contemporary American Culture', Daedalus, Sept. 1957.

[5] S. de Grazia, *Of Time, Work and Leisure,* New York: Twentieth Century Fund, 1962, p. 246.

[6] J. Dumazedier and N. Latouche, 'Work and Leisure in French Sociology', *Industrial Relations*, Feb. 1962.

[7] S. de Grazia, *op. cit.*

work and leisure respectively, but both are *dimensions* of work *and* leisure. Unless this two-dimensional property of work and leisure is appreciated, it is impossible to understand that work (or leisure) is a quality of activity which only problematically and not necessarily takes place within a space of time labelled work (or leisure).

VARIABLES AFFECTING THE RELATIONSHIP

The ways in which work and leisure are interrelated are partly a matter of the personality characteristics of the individuals concerned, partly a result of cultural patterns which influence general behaviour norms, and partly a function of the occupation which an individual follows. Personality is of more central concern to psychologists; the cultural influences, although matters of interest to sociologists, would take us outside the scope of this book; but the sub-cultural influences of occupation *are* relevant.

Data are available on the relation between work and leisure characteristic of a wide variety of occupational groups. Dealing first with the manual group, the decreased physical strain of work has brought about a change in the function of leisure for some manual workers. Thus it has been observed that the jobs of steel workers have now become so relatively lacking in strain that the worker leaves the plant with a good deal of energy to spare, which carries him readily through his leisure hours.[8] However, with industries like mining and farming leisure tends to have a very traditional quality. Tunstall's study of distant-water fishermen showed that leisure during the three months in the year they are ashore fulfils the functions of status seeking and of explosive compensation for physically damaging work.[9]

Something of this reaction to work can be seen in the leisure activities of some non-manual workers. Friedmann quotes a study of the leisure occupations of employees at the Postal Cheque Centre in Paris, whose jobs are completely routine: on leaving the office these clerks are either much more active or, on the countrary, withdraw into themselves in a sort of apathy.[10] But a different pattern of work and leisure is shown by those non-manual employees whose work demands more involvement and responsibility. From their survey, Heckscher and DeGrazia report that the way of life of the American business execu-

[8] D. Riesman, 'Some Observations on Changes in Leisure Attitudes', *Antioch Review*, No. 4, 1952.

[9] J. Tunstall, *The Fishermen*, London: MacGibbon and Kee, 1962, p. 137.

[10] G. Friedmann, 'Leisure and Technological Civilization', *International Social Science Journal*, No. 4, 1960.

tive permits no clear-cut distinction between work and leisure.[11] To counteract the encroachment of work on leisure time, the executive's work is penetrated by qualities which we would normally associate with leisure.

The penetration of the businessmen's work into the rest of his life is a function of the demands of the work itself rather than of the culture, and Vogel shows the close similarity of the Japanese businessman's life to that of the American.[12] He also notes that, like successful businessmen, doctors rarely make a sharp separation between work and leisure, partly because to some extent working hours are determined by the arrival of patients. It is the salaried man who makes the sharpest distinction between working time and free time. In contrast to the businessman who mixes business and leisure, and to the doctor whose leisure is determined by the absence of patients, the salaried man generally has set hours so that he can plan certain hours of the day and certain days of the week for himself and his family.

Some French sociologists have done empirical work on the relation between work and leisure. In the preface to a study of pigeon cultivation among miners, Friedmann pointed out that leisure does more than merely offer a compensation for the technique of work.[13] It brings professional compensations for work with a limited horizon, emotional compensations for the crudity of social relations in mass society, and social compensations through the success which this leisure-time activity can provide. After quoting this study, Dumazedier and Latouche note that, far from being a compensation, leisure is more often only an extension of occupational life. They refer to a study by Louchet showing that there is a tendency for the most frustrating leisure to be associated with the most frustrating work.

Several studies provide evidence of the relation between satisfaction at work and attitudes and values of leisure. Among a sample of South African adults, du Toit reported that those who found more satisfaction in their leisure than in their work had a relatively negative attitude toward their work, and vice versa.[14] In the city of Kuwait, research showed that those who were dissatisfied with their jobs tended to be more active in leisure pursuits than those who were relatively

[11] A. Heckscher and S. de Grazia, 'Executive Leisure', *Harvard Business Review*, July 1959.

[12] E. F. Vogel, *Japan's New Middle Class*, Berkeley: University of California Press, 1963, p. 21.

[13] J. Dumazedier and N. Latouche, *op. cit.*

[14] J. B. DuToit, 'Work and Leisure Roles of Young People', *Sociology and Social Research*, March 1960.

satisfied.[15] In his study of workers in the French town of Annecy, Dumazedier observed a slight tendency for the worker who expressed satisfaction with work to attach less importance to certain semi-leisure activities centred in the home, such as family festivals.[16] It is among the workers who find their work interesting that intellectual curiosity and the need for complementary education are most lively. Those who are satisfied with their work tend to assume more *responsibilities* in associations of all kinds, except political action groups, where more who are not interested in their work are found.

TOWARDS A THEORY OF WORK AND LEISURE

There are broadly two schools of thought on the relation of spheres of life in urban-industrial society. The first—who may be called segmentalists—hold that society is continuously subdivided into areas of activity and interest, with each social segment lived out more or less independently of the rest.[17] Work is separated from leisure, production from consumption, workplace from residence, education from religion, politics from recreation.[18] The second school—the 'holists'—maintain that society is now moving toward a fusion of work and leisure. Work, they claim, is now becoming more like play, and play more like work. Attitudes and practices developed in one sphere of life can spill over into another—killing time at work can become killing time in leisure, apathy in the workplace can become apathy in politics, alienation from one, alienation from the other.

The 'fusion' versus 'polarity' hypotheses can be tested against developments in work content, organization and environment. Wilensky cites as evidence of work-leisure fusion the long coffee break among white-collar girls, the lunch 'hour' among top business and professional people, card games among night shift employees; and off work, the do-it-yourself movement, spare-time jobs, 'customers' golf' for sales executives, and commuter-train conferences for account executives.[19] Also, many devices are being invented for creating spaces of free time during the working day and at intervals through the career. In America the sabbatical year is no longer exclusive to academic

[15] A. Matthews and B. Abu-Laban, 'Job Satisfaction and Leisure-Time Activity', *Sociology and Social Research*, Jan. 1959.

[16] J. Dumazedier and N. Latouche, *op. cit.*

[17] R. Dubin, 'Industrial Workers' Worlds', *Social Problems*, Jan. 1956.

[18] H. Wilensky, 'Work, Careers and Social Integration', *International Social Science Journal*, No. 4, 1960.

[19] H. Wilensky, 'Mass Society and Mass Culture: Interdependence or Independence?', *American Sociological Review*, April 1964.

employees. One firm has for some time ben granting twelve months paid holiday after ten years of service.[20]

There are others, however, who take a different view. Dismissing evidence of fusion such as that cited above as peripheral to the main structure of modern industry, they seek to show that work has become more concentratedly and actively work. Work may be less arduous physically than it used to be, they say, but its present standards of efficiency require one to key oneself to a higher pitch of nervous and mental effort.[21] The theme of alienation from work is relevant here, since it implies that work as a sphere of human experience is estranged from other spheres such as those of leisure. Under conditions of present society, the 'break in consciousness' between work and socialized play, begun during the industrial revolution, has been completed.[22]

The evidence is conflicting and the theories built on selections of it are not easily reconcilable. Perhaps the whole fusion versus polarity argument has been carried on at the too general level of society when it should have been applied to the sub-cultural level of occupations and work milieux. With this in mind, the present writer carried out a study of three occupational groups at broadly the same class-status level, but who differ substantially in the kinds of work they do.[23]

Questionnaires were sent to samples of employees in banking, youth employment and child care.[24] Results showed that the bank people typically felt that in their work they used only some of their abilities in a general way; the majority of the child care officers felt that they used most of their abilities in quite an intensive way; and the youth employment officers felt that they used most of their abilities but without a clear-cut degree of intensity. The main sources of satisfaction differed in the three occupations. The bank people most often found their jobs satisfying because of security or 'pleasant people to work with' ('extrinsic' factors). The youth employment and child care people most often gained satisfaction from 'interesting work' or 'the chance to help clients' ('intrinsic' factors).

[20] A. Rubner, *Fringe Benefits*, London: Putnam, 1962, p. 26.

[21] C. Greenberg, 'Work and Leisure under Industrialism', in E. Larrabee and R. Meyersohn (eds.), *Mass Leisure*, Glencoe: Free Press, 1958.

[22] This line of argument is developed by A. W. Green (*Recreation, Leisure and Politics*, New York: McGraw-Hill, 1964, pp. 171–2), who does not appear to subscribe to it himself.

[23] S. R. Parker, 'Work and Non-Work in Three Occupations', *Sociological Review*, March 1965.

[24] The designed sample was 250 employees in each occupation and the overall response was 46%, giving 344 respondents.

Information was obtained on the amount of leisure which people in the three occupations had. Some respondents found it difficult to estimate their amount of leisure time, and it was clear that definitions of what constitutes leisure vary considerably.[25] However, the differences between occupational groups were comparatively unaffected by the problem of definition. The bank people reported having an average of forty-two hours of leisure a week, against about thirty-four hours for the other two groups.

Another set of questions in the survey sought to gain information on the relative importance which individuals in certain occupations give to work and leisure spheres in their life pattern. The following patterns emerged:[26] (1) The bank employees characteristically enjoy leisure because it is completely different from work, do not have much of their free time taken up by things connected with their work, and have their central life interest in the family sphere, with leisure second, and (2) the child care and youth employment people characteristically enjoy leisure because it is satisfying in a different way from work, have a lot of their free time taken up by things connected with their work, and more often have their central life interest in work.

From these survey results, interpreted in the light of previous research on other occupational groups, it appears that there may be three typical ways in which people tend to relate their work to their leisure:
(1) The *extension* pattern consists of having leisure activities which are often similar in content to one's working activities, making no sharp distinction between what is considered work and what is considered leisure, and having one's central life interest in work rather than in family or leisure spheres. This pattern seems to be associated with certain work factors: a high degree of autonomy in the work situation, use of most abilities in the work, high—or, in Etzioni's terms, 'moral'—involvement in the work, and intrinsic satisfaction derived from it. People who exhibit this pattern are likely to have rather little time for activities which they define as leisure, which functions for them mainly as development of personality, and they are probably well-educated. Typical occupations which seem to be associated with this pattern are those of successful businessmen, doctors, teachers, some skilled manual workers, and social workers, especially the kind who live and work on the same premises.
(2) The *neutrality* pattern consists of having leisure activities which

[25] A few respondents obviously deducted their standard working week from the 168 hours in a week to arrive at a total of leisure hours.

[26] These are discussed more fully in relation to wider issues in S. R. Parker, *The Future of Work and Leisure*, MacGibbon and Kee, 1971.

are somewhat different from work, making a distinction between work and leisure, and having one's central life interest in family or leisure rather than in the work sphere. The work factors associated with this pattern are: medium to low degree of autonomy in the work situation, use of only some abilities in the work, indifferent or 'calculative' involvement in the work, and satisfaction found in extrinsic work factors. In the non-work sphere these individuals are likely to have fairly long hours of leisure, which functions for them chiefly as relaxation, and they have an average level of education. Typical occupations associated with this pattern are those of clerical workers, semi-skilled manual workers, and minor professionals other than social workers.

(3) With the *opposition* pattern leisure activities are definitely unlike work, there is a sharp demarcation between work and leisure, and central life interest is in the non-work sphere. The associated work factors are: low degree of autonomy in the work situation, use of only a narrow range of abilities, hostile or 'alienative' attitude towards work, and satisfaction (if any) found in extrinsic work factors. In the non-work sphere, the hours of leisure are likely to be long (though perhaps less regular than with the neutrality pattern), the chief function of leisure is recuperation from work, and the level of education is generally low. Although this pattern is to some extent exhibited by routine clerical workers, it seems more typical of unskilled manual workers, and those in occupations such as mining and distant-water fishing.

Considerably more research needs to be done to test the validity of these provisional findings. Although the 'problem of leisure', if this means knowing what to do with a sharp increase in non-work time, is unlikely to affect the mass of people in the near future, there are several special groups that it is already affecting. Earlier retirement and a longer expectation of life are combining to give more time without employment to many people. Technical developments in some industries are changing the distribution of, as well as shortening the traditional hours of work, involving four or even three-day working weeks for some. Unfortunately, as Wilensky has pointed out, those who have most leisure time seem to have least resources for its creative use.[27] A knowledge of the ways in which work and leisure are interrelated helps us to understand that the problems of leisure are not likely to be successfully tackled without some consideration of the quality and meaning of working life.

[27] H. Wilensky, *op. cit.*

Sociological Enquiry and the Study of Industry

THIS concluding chapter briefly considers two main strategies through which sociological enquiry may be related to the study of industry. The first derives from the frame of reference of sociology as a whole. It adopts the view (discussed in Chapter 1) that industrial sociology is a particular level from which generalizations applicable to sociology as a whole are derived, as well as to which they are applied.[1] The second strategy takes for its point of departure the study of industry, or organizational activity in general, as a particular empirically defined area. The study of organizations is regarded as a quasi-independent science which is currently emerging to claim academic attention in its own right. This study draws upon and contributes to all the social sciences, as well as relevant aspects of engineering technology. These two strategies, while distinctive, are by no means mutually exclusive.

INDUSTRY AND SOCIOLOGICAL CONTINUITIES

It is apparent that much of the research reviewed in previous chapters relates closely to some of the most important continuities within sociology. This illustrates the first strategy, to which this book has inclined by giving prominence to the thesis that industrial sociology is integral with sociology in general, sharing the same theoretical assumptions and problems, possessing parallel aims and content. We shall take four examples of subjects of enquiry and debate which may serve to clarify this point. These are (i) the relationship of the economic system to other systems within society and to configurations of social structure as a whole; (ii) the social bases for conflict and consensus; (iii) the question of alienation in modern society; and (iv) the methodological problem of values in social investigation.

[1] E. V. Schneider, *Industrial Sociology*, New York: McGraw-Hill 1957, p. 5.

(i) Discussion of the role of economic forces in social development, particularly the argument that such forces cause social structure to pass through similar evolutionary stages culminating in the same structural configuration, is primarily associated with Marx.[2] Although general theories of social evolution are largely discredited today, evidence that technological and economic factors tend to fashion the structure of industrial organizations in similar ways across different societies has encouraged the exposition of a modern adaptation of Marx—the so-called 'convergence' thesis. This thesis, as advanced by a number of American sociologists, implies that factors working towards uniformity in industrial societies tend to override those making for inter-societal differences, such as dissimilar national cultures and political systems. It is suggested therefore that as countries reach a stage of advanced industrialization their social systems and major institutions become increasingly comparable.[3] Galbraith has recently re-stated this argument, linking supposed convergent tendencies between industrial societies to their common need to plan consumption patterns, income distribution, manpower and technological development, within their economies.[4] Although the process of industrial development may impose certain common material exigencies upon social systems, evidence has been brought to indicate that, with regard to social stratification at least, purposive action through the medium of educational, economic and other policy has had considerable influence on the shaping of social structure. Such action has in turn been associated with cultural values and ideologies peculiar to particular societies.[5]

(ii) The social bases for conflict and consensus within work organizations are directly comparable to those active in society as a whole. It has been argued in previous chapters that work organizations contain structures designed to utilize the contributions of individuals towards a set of common purposes, but that such structures coexist with systems of differential power, status and other rewards which are condu-

[2] T. B. Bottomore and M. Rubel (eds.), *Karl Marx—Seclected Writings in Sociology and Social Philosophy*, London: Watts, 1956, Part One, Section 1.

[3] J. H. Goldthorpe, 'Social Stratification in Industrial Society', in P. Halmos (ed.), *The Development of Industrial Societies*, Sociological Review Monograph No. 8, 1964, esp. pp. 97–103.

[4] J. K. Galbraith, 1966 Reith Lectures, *The Listener*, 17th November–22nd December 1966.

[5] J. H. Goldthorpe, *op. cit.* and the following discussion by J. A. Platt; E. G. Dunning and E. I. Hopper, 'Industrialization and the Problem of Convergence: a Critical Note', *Sociological Review*, July 1966, pp. 163–186, and reply by J. H. Goldthorpe, pp. 187–195.

cive to varying degrees and types of conflict and rivalry. Research into social behaviour in industry has indicated the weakness of the mainly managerial theories which assumed an exclusive state of social consensus and a single system of goals to represent the 'normal' condition of organizations. Similarly, at the level of society as a whole, opposed theories of conflict and consensus have today to a large extent been reconciled by the realization that a society as such would be unthinkable without some minimum normative consensus among its members, but that such consensus is at the same time compatible with sectional rivalry for social rewards and gratifications, and with adherence to different sub-cultures possessing their own distinct values and goals.[6]

(iii) The concept of 'alienation' was discussed in Chapter 13. It has commonly been used to embrace both attributes of roles in terms of their inability to afford meaning, control and social integration to occupants, as well as the consequent subjective experience of individuals in terms of non-involvement and self-estrangement. The theme of alienation formed part of Marx's critique of the excessive division of labour in capitalist society. This, Marx argued, caused the worker to lose control over the conditions and the fruits of his labour and led him to estrangement both from himself and his fellow men.[7] Veblen associated the predominant role of business enterprise in western society with a financial manipulation of industry detrimental to what he considered to be a universal trait in man—the 'instinct of workmanship'.[8] For Marx and Veblen, alienation was a consequence of the capitalist economic system. Weber, however, linked alienating tendencies with the phenomenon of bureaucratization, which he envisaged as a structural concomitant of any developed industrial society. He regarded the separation of workers from the means of production as but a particular case which had to be set alongside a similar administrative development within the civil service, the military and the universities.[9]

Blauner has indicated how the various dimensions of alienation in work situations vary in form and intensity according to the industrial setting. Although there may be some general alienating features in

[6] T. Burns, 'On the Plurality of Social Systems' in J. R. Lawrence (ed.), *Operational Research and the Social Sciences*, London: Tavistock 1966, p. 165; D. Lockwood, 'Some Remarks on "The Social System" ', *British Journal of Sociology*, June 1956, pp. 134–146.

[7] T. B. Bottomore and M. Rubel (eds.), *op. cit.*, Part Three, Section IV.

[8] T. Veblen, *The Theory of Business Enterprise*, New York: Scribners, 1904.

[9] H. H. Gerth and C. W. Mills (eds.), *From Max Weber—Essays in Sociology*, London: Routledge, 1948, pp. 49–50 and Chapter VIII.

modern production techniques and bureaucratic industrial organization, their incidence will tend to vary according to prevailing technology, division of labour, economic structure and industrial social organization.[10] Also it is now recognized that, within broad limits set by technology, there exists scope for the modification of work roles to provide greater subjective meaning for their occupants.[11] Regarding the subjective experience of people at work, it is important to distinguish between alienation (referring to the relation between individuals and the nature of their work) and satisfaction (referring to the relation between expectations and rewards).[12] For instance, there is evidence that where intrinsic and social rewards are not readily obtained at work, many employees are still willing to undertake this work and to use its favourable material rewards as an 'instrument' towards the fulfilment of their ambitions in the non-work sphere. In effect, the expectations and rewards of work for such employees centre around its extrinsic contributions, and this allows some satisfactions to be derived from employment where work is of an alienating nature.[13]

Although there are possibilities for the re-structuring of work roles to mitigate their alienating features, the incidence of alienation from work may still be extending today with, for example, the bureaucratization of clerical activities and the growing scale of organizations. And even if satisfying material rewards are available for undertaking this work, it is possible that (at a more fundamental level) the low intrinsic quality of work life with which many people are faced in routine jobs may impair their personal resources for the 'creative' use of leisure and for the development of effective social relationships outside work. This is an area requiring further research, and touching as it does on notions such as 'mental health', it is particularly susceptible to value-judgements.

(iv) The place of values in social investigation is, in fact, our fourth example of a continuing sociological concern which has had particular bearing on the study of industry. Weber's views on this problem are today probably accepted by the great majority of British sociologists. He carefully distinguished between the legitimate role of values in the

[10] R. Blauner, *Alienation and Freedom*, Chicago: University Press, 1964.

[11] E. L. Trist *et al.*, *Organizational Choice*, London: Tavistock, 1963; G. Friedmann, *The Anatomy of Work*, London: Heinemann, 1961, esp. Chapters III and IV.

[12] A. Touraine *et al.*, *Workers' Attitudes to Technical Change*, Paris: OECD, 1965, pp. 16–21.

[13] J. H. Goldthorpe, 'Attitudes and Behaviour of Car Assembly Workers: a Deviant Case and a Theoretical Critique', *British Journal of Sociology*, September 1966, pp. 227–244.

selection of subjects for scientific study, and the illegitimate exercise of value judgements in the formulation of conclusions about the causes and consequences of phenomena being studied.[14] The problem of the intrusion of values upon the work of social scientists is by now long recognized, although some controversy still attaches to the question of how far a 'value-free' social science may be attained.[15] So far as industry is concerned, the plurality of interests and goals which it encompasses has been stressed in previous chapters. The implication which follows is that any objectively valid analysis in industrial sociology must recognize that alternative values are present within work organizations, and that it must consequently beware of exclusively accepting assumptions deriving from the orientation of any single party to industrial life. As was noted in Chapter 9, early work in industrial sociology falling within the 'human relations' school has been severely criticized for offering partial explanations of observed phenomena, the partiality in most cases being attributable to the adoption of an exclusively managerial point of view towards industrial behaviour.

The first strategy relating sociological enquiry to the study of industry will continue to focus on questions of central concern to the development of sociological analysis as a whole. Regarding the study of advanced industrial societies, Rex has recently listed a number of such questions which are now engaging the attention of sociologists—'Is it the case that advanced capitalist societies have solved their major problems of economic and political stability? Is it the case that the working-class has now been successfully "incorporated" into the value-system . . . ? Is there a common level of mobility which is achieved by all societies at a certain level of industrial advancement? In what ways are the motivations of owners, managers and workers tied into the organization of the modern corporation?'[16] Other areas of future research falling within this strategy are likely to include the relationship between different patterns of work and leisure (with an emphasis on the question of how people's overall 'quality of life' is influenced by their work experience), and the relative influence of cultural and technological factors in the structuring of organizational behaviour and orientations in different societies.

[14] T. Parsons, *The Structure of Social Action*, Glencoe: Free Press, 1949, pp. 593–594.

[15] Cf., A. W. Gouldner, 'Anti-Minotaur: the Myth of a Value-Free Sociology' in M. Stein and A. Vidich (eds.), *Sociology on Trial*, Englewood Cliffs: Prentice-Hall 1963, pp. 35–52.

[16] J. Rex, 'Which Path for Sociology?', *New Society*, October 6, 1966, p. 529.

'ORGANIZATION THEORY'

The second strategy linking sociological enquiry and the study of industry often passes under this heading. This concentrates on the study of the structure and functioning of organizations (including non-industrial ones) and on the behaviour of groups and individuals within them. This new sub-discipline makes use of concepts drawn from management theorists, students of organization structure, social psychologists, industrial psychologists, economic theorists, and technology theorists.[17] Sociology is thus but one contributory discipline to the development of 'organization theory', which despite its title does not as yet have a fully integrated theoretical framework and is predominantly empirical in its orientation.

The organization theory strategy has the great merit of seeking to reach an understanding of structure, behaviour and attitudes through utilizing all the social sciences together, albeit within a restricted empirical area. It can thus benefit from all their various insights and methods of investigation as and when appropriate. An open system approach to explanation is coming to be favoured by many researchers within this field, and it has the advantage of drawing attention to the relations between action and context at any level of analysis. In this way it serves to highlight the continuum of explanation running from the level of individual personality dynamics through to the functioning of whole societies in their inter-social context. The three constituent parts of this book have in fact been concerned with a section of this continuum—ranging from the level of person-role interaction, through the role-organization level, to the institution-social system level.

Students of industry are slowly granting greater recognition to an analytical continuum of this nature, which is part and parcel of the inter-disciplinary approach utilized by organization theory. Thus a new field, 'organizational psychology', is emerging which should provide a connection with the work of technology theorists and students of organization structure.[18] Links are being forged between economists and sociologists through studies of 'managerial capitalism' and through the study of organization functioning within its socio-economic

[17] D. S. Pugh, 'Modern Organization Theory: a Psychological and Sociological Study', *Psychological Bulletin*, October 1966, pp. 235–251.

[18] R. Cooper, 'The Psychology of Organizations', *New Society*, April 22, 1965, pp. 14–17; D. Katz and R. L. Kahn, *The Social Psychology of Organizations*, New York: Wiley, 1966.

context.[19] These are some of the areas of research engaging those working primarily within this second strategy. It can readily be seen that such research is equally concerned with some of the most fundamental questions facing society today, including the search for organizational efficiency and the anticipation of the human problems associated with emerging forms of technology.

19 E.g., R. Marris, *The Economic Theory of 'Managerial' Capitalism*, London: Macmillan, 1964; J. Child, *The Business Enterprise in Modern Industrial Society*, London: Collier-Macmillan, 1969.

Selected Further Reading

(Place of publication is London unless otherwise stated)

PART I

There are no British textbooks covering substantially the whole area of industrial sociology as defined widely in this book. J. A. Banks, 'The Sociology of Work' (in T. R. Fyvel (ed.), *The Frontiers of Sociology*, Cohen and West, 1964) is a good brief review of some typical problems, and T. Burns, 'The Sociology of Industry' (in A. T. Welford (ed.), *Society: Problems and Methods of Study*, Routledge, 1962) is an excellent summary of theory and research. Several American textbooks may be recommended on theoretical grounds, despite the limited use of illustrative material to non-American readers. These include E. V. Schneider, *Industrial Sociology* (New York: McGraw-Hill, 1969), D. C. Miller and W. H. Form, *Industrial Sociology* (New York: Harper and Row, 1963, reprinted in a cheapter edition 1964), and W. E. Moore, *Industrial Relations and the Social Order* (New York: Macmillan, 1951).

Probably the best concise theoretical work on the economical subsystem is N. J. Smelser, *The Sociology of Economic Life* (Englewood Cliffs: Prentice-Hall, 1963). P. Sargant Florence, *Economics and Sociology of Industry* (Watts, 1969) contains a useful discussion of trends in the British economy, although not much sociological analysis. Official statistics are summarized in chapters in A. M. Carr-Saunders *et al., A Survey of Social Conditions in England and Wales* (Oxford University Press, 1958), which can be brought up to date with 1961 Census data. Other reference works include G. C. Allen, *The Structure of Industry in Britain* (Longmans, 1966) and E. V.

Morgan, *The Structure of Property Ownership in Great Britain* (Oxford: Clarendon Press, 1960).

Several chapters on aspects of industry and education are in A. H. Halsey *et al., Education, Economy and Society* (Glencoe: Free Press, 1961). The transition from school to work is dealt with in M. P. Carter, *Home, School and Work* (Oxford: Pergamon Press, 1962) and T. Veness, *School Leavers* (Methuen, 1962). S. Cotgrove, *Technical Education and Social Change* (Allen and Unwin, 1958) gives a critical account of the history and present position of technical education, and G. Williams, *Recruitment to Skilled Trades* (Routledge, 1957) does the same for apprenticeship.

Much of the material on industry and the family is contained in the American journals, of which R. and R. Rapoport, 'Work and Family in Contemporary Society' (*American Sociological Review*, June 1965) is an outstanding theoretical contribution. R. O. Blood and D. M. Wolfe, *Husbands and Wives* (Glencoe: Free Press, 1960) and D. C. McKinley, *Social Class and Family Life* (Glencoe: Free Press, 1964) both deal with work and family variables. One of the few British books which throw light on this subject is E. Bott, *Family and Social Network* (Tavistock, 1957). V. Klein, *Britain's Married Women Workers* (Routledge, 1965) is a useful collection of articles.

Class and status as forms of stratification based on economic position are dealt with generally in T. B. Bottomore, *Classes in Modern Society* (Allen and Unwin, 1965) and R. Dahrendorf, *Class and Class Conflict in an Industrial Society* (Routledge, 1959), and more specifically in relation to occupational groups in D. Lockwood, *The Blackcoated Worker* (Allen and Unwin, 1958) and K. Prandy, *Professional Employees* (Faber and Faber, 1965). British material on occupational status is contained in articles in the *British Journal of Sociology*: J. Hall and D. Jones, 'Social Grading of Occupations', (Mar. 1950) and M. Young and P. Willmott, 'Social Grading by Manual Workers', (Dec. 1956).

British sources on the relation of industry and the community are very few and scattered (see footnotes to Chapter 6 for some). The theory of industry-community relations is dealt with in W. H. Form and D. C. Miller, *Industry, Labor and Community* (New York: Harper, 1960). Aspects of the industrial influence on politics and the political constraints on industry are discussed respectively in J. D. Stewart, *British Pressure Groups* (Oxford: Clarendon Press, 1958) and J. W. Grove, *Government and Industry in Britain* (Longmans, 1962). K. W. Wedderburn, *The Worker and the Law* (MacGibbon and Kee, 1966) is a good recent work in its field.

PART II

Most of the extensive published work on organization theory is American; a useful introduction is C. Perrow, *Organizational Analysis; A Sociological View* (Tavistock, 1970). Other studies include C. Argyris, *Integrating the Individual and the Organization* (New York: Wiley, 1964), P. M. Blau and W. R. Scott, *Formal Organizations* (Routledge, 1963) and A. Etzioni, *A Comparative Analysis of Complex Organizations* (Glencoe: Free Press, 1961). For an examination of the concept of role and its application to work analysis see R. L. Kahn *et al.*, *Organizational Stress* (New York: Wiley, 1964). Several readers are available in the subject, notably A. Etzioni, *Complex Organizations: A Sociological Reader* (New York: Holt, Rinehart, 1969) and J. G. March, *Handbook of Organizations* (Chicago: Rand, McNally, 1965).

Literature on management also abounds, much of it dealing with the problems of management rather than with its sociology. W. B. D. Brown, *Exploration in Management* (Heinemann, 1960) is an instructive case study. Academic works include J. Child, *The Business Enterprise in Modern Industrial Society* (Collier-Macmillan, 1969), T. Lupton, *Management and the Social Sciences* (Hutchinson, 1966), R. Stewart, *Managers and Their Jobs* (Macmillan, 1967), and J. Woodward, *Industrial Organization* (Oxford University Press, 1970). Of American books, M. Dalton, *Men who Manage* (New York: Wiley, 1959) focuses on problem areas, while F. Harbison and C. A. Myers, *Management in the Industrial World* (New York: McGraw-Hill, 1959) is an international analysis.

A good introduction to the development of the Human Relations movement and studies of the working group is G. Friedmann, *Industrial Society* (Glencoe: Free Press, 1955). The full account of the Hawthorne Experiments is F. J. Roethlisberger and W. J. Dickson, *Management and the Worker* (Cambridge, Mass.: Harvard University Press, 1939). Two books by Elton Mayo have had great influence, *The Human Problems of an Industrial Civilization* (New York: Macmillan, 1933) and *The Social Problems of an Industrial Civilization* (Routledge, 1949). H. A. Landsberger, *Hawthorne Revisited* (Ithaca, N.Y.: Cornell University Press, 1958) provides a balanced account of the Hawthorne studies and of much of the subsequent criticism. Two notable studies of working groups are L. R. Sayles, *Behaviour of Industrial Work Groups* (New York: Wiley, 1958), and T. Lupton, *On the Shop Floor* (Oxford: Pergamon, 1963).

A valuable collection of readings on technology and technical change is C. R. Walker (ed.), *Modern Technology and Civilization* (New York:

McGraw-Hill, 1962). Studies of technical change in a steel works are reported in W. H. Scott *et al.*, *Technical Change and Industrial Relations*, and O. Banks, *The Attitudes of Steelworkers to Technical Change* (Liverpool: University Press 1956 and 1960), and related issues discussed in T. Burns and G. M. Stalker, *The Management of Innovation* (Tavistock, 1960) and A. Touraine *et al.*, *Workers' Attitudes to Technical Change* (Paris: OECD, 1965). Books on the social consequences of automation soon get out of date, but recent ones include L. C. Hunter *et al.*, *Labour Problems of Technological Change* (Allen and Unwin, 1970) and S. Marcson, *Automation, Alienation, and Anomie* (New York: Harper, 1970).

Among the many books on British trade unions the most comprehensive is B. C. Roberts, *Trade Union Government and Administration* (Bell, 1956). H. Clegg, (ed.), *The System of Industrial Relations in Great Britain* (Oxford: Blackwell, 1970) is a useful collection of essays. A case study with some consideration of theory is W. H. Scott *et al.*, *Coal and Conflict* (Liverpool: University Press, 1963). The research papers for the *Royal Commission on Trade Unions and Employers' Associations* (HMSO, 1966-68) include up-to-date empirical material. American contributions are generally more theoretical and include R. Dubin, *Working Union-Management Relations* (Englewood Cliffs: Prentice-Hall, 1958), J. T. Dunlop, *Industrial Relations Systems* (New York: Holt, 1958) and A. Kornhauser *et al.*, (eds.), *Industrial Conflict* (New York: McGraw-Hill, 1954).

PART III

Most books on the sociology of work and occupations are American. T. Caplow, *The Sociology of Work* (Minneapolis: University of Minnesota Press, 1954) covers most aspects of the subject, and a good reader is S. Nosow and W. H. Form (eds.), *Man, Work and Society* (New York: Basic Books, 1962). On mobility, N. Rogoff, *Recent Trends in Occupational Mobility* (Glencoe: Free Press, 1953) and H. S. Parnes, *Research on Labor Mobility* (New York: Social Science Research Council Bulletin, 1954) are good theoretical and empirical works; for British data the two Government Social Survey reports should be consulted (see Chapter 12).

Books wholly devoted to various aspects of the subjective experience of work are all American. On work ideologies there is R. Bendix, *Work and Authority in Industry* (New York: Wiley, 1957); on values and occupational choice, M. Rosenberg *et al.*, *Occupations and Values* (Glencoe: Free Press, 1957); on alienation, R. Blauner, *Alienation and Freedom* (Chicago: University Press, 1954); on the meaning of work, E. A. Friedmann and R. J. Havighurst, *The Meaning of Work and Retirement* (Chicago: University Press, 1954); and on motivation and satisfaction, F. Herzberg *et al.*, *The Motivation to Work* (New York: Wiley, 1959). P. L. Berger (ed.), *The Human Shape of Work* (New York: Macmillan, 1964) is a collection of articles dealing with attitudes of a number of occupational groups.

Books on work and leisure are few, even in America. N. Anderson, *Work and Leisure* (Routledge, 1961) brings together a wide variety of research findings and more general observations; E. O. Smigel (ed.), *Work and Leisure* (New Haven: College and University Press) is a collection of articles. Research and theoretical considerations are discussed in S. R. Parker, *The Future of Work and Leisure* (MacGibbon and Kee, 1971).

INDEX

GEORGE ALLEN & UNWIN LTD

Head Office
40 Museum Street, London W.C.1
Telephone: 01-405 8577
Sales, Distribution and Accounts Departments
Park Lane, Hemel Hempstead, Herts.
Telephone: 0442 3244

Athens: 7 Stadiou Street, Athens 125
Auckland: P.O. Box 36013, Auckland 9
Barbados: Rockley New Road, St Lawrence 4
Bombay: 103/5 Fort Street, Bombay 1
Calcutta: 285J Bepin Behari Ganguli Street, Calcutta 12
Dacca: Alico Building, 18 Motijheel, Dacca 2
Hornsby, N.S.W.: Cnr. Bridge Road and Jersey Street, 2077
Ibadan: P.O. Box 62
Johannesburg: P.O. Box 23134, Joubert Park
Karachi: Karachi Chambers, McLeod Road, Karachi 2
Lahore: 22 Falettis' Hotel, Egerton Road
Madras: 2/18 Mount Road, Madras 2
Manila: P.O. Box 157, Quezon City, D-502
Mexico: Serapio Rendon 125, Mexico 4, D.F.
Nairobi: P.O. Box 30583
New Delhi: 4/21-22B Asaf Ali Road, New Delhi 1
Ontario: 2330 Midland Avenue, Agincourt
Singapore: 248C-6 Orchard Road, Singapore 9
Tokyo: C.P.O. Box 1728, Tokyo 100-91

SOCIAL WORK AND SOCIAL VALUES

COMPILED BY DAME EILEEN YOUNGHUSBAND

This volume of the *Readings in Social Work* series will appeal especially to social workers, administrators, social work teachers and those who are becoming increasingly concerned about the whole question of value assumptions in social work. So far little has been written on a subject of lively discussion amongst practitioners and students alike; in this volume are gathered together some of the most influential and often quoted articles which have appeared in Britain and the United States in recent years. They deal not only with the general ethics of professional practice and specific situations but also with conflicting value judgments in administrative settings and the relation between administration and values.

THE SCIENCE OF SOCIETY

STEPHEN COTGROVE

The emphasis throughout is on the sociological study of industrial society, with particular reference to modern England. After an introductory discussion of sociological perspectives, there are chapters on each of the major sub-systems of society; the family, the educational system, the economy, the political system and belief systems. The book ends with three chapters on major social processes; social differentiation and stratification, organization, and finally, social change, including a discussion of deviancy and disorganization.

This text should prove to be of particular value not only to university students, but also to the rapidly growing number studying sociology in colleges of education and technical colleges, and those attending the more advanced adult education and extra-mural classes. Each chapter ends with questions and exercises, together with a bibliography of the major texts. Extensive footnotes direct the attention of students to articles and books for the more intensive study of particular topics.

Dr Cotgrove is a graduate of the London School of Economics, and is now Professor of Sociology at Bath University of Technology. He is the author of *Technical Education and Social Change*, and of a number of articles on the education and employment of technicians and scientists.

GEORGE ALLEN & UNWIN LTD